Sh*tty Mom

FOR ALL SEASONS

Sh*tty Mom

FOR ALL SEASONS

HALF-@SSING IT ALL YEAR LONG

ALICIA YBARBO AND
MARY ANN ZOELLNER,
WITH ERIN CLUNE

ABRAMS IMAGE, NEW YORK

CONTENTS

Introduction 8

SECTION ONE: SPRING

1 Finding Your Lost Kids and Other Practical Spring Break Advice 11

2 The Coolest Birthday Party Ideas Ever for Moms Who Really, *Really* Love Their Kids! 18

3 Beat Your Rugs, Not Your Relatives: Spring-Cleaning Your Way to Personal Happiness 21

4 Matzo Balls, Lambs, and Locusts, Oh My! Whatever You Do This Holiday Season, Don't Get on the Neighborhood Listserv 25

5 Mean Girls Yoga: Signs Your Spring Exercise Regimen Isn't Right for You 30

6 Mommy's Running Off with the Gardener: April Fools'! 34

7 Moms with Girls: Psycho BFFs 38

8 Moms with Boys: Broken Bones 41

9 Mayday! Mayday! Mayday! Weathering the Last Month of School 44

SECTION TWO: SUMMER

10 School's Out. Nobody Panic! 49

11 Sorting Through the Stuff Your Kids Brought Home from School, Then Throwing Most of It Away 55

12 Suggestions for Summer Vacations #1: Riding the Rails 59

13 Suggestions for Summer Vacations #2: Visiting Relatives 62

14 Suggestions for Summer Vacations #3: Camping 66

15 Should I Have Had *One More*? No. And That Baby Hates You. 69

16 Go Away, Kid: How to Make Sure Your "Homesick" Kid Goes to Camp 74

17 The Fourth of July for Kids: Lessons About America They Don't Teach in School 78

18 Help! My Babysitter Sucks! 81

19 This Is Why You Don't Homeschool: The Summer Reading List and Other Hallucinations 85

20 Your Only Goal Is Getting There: The Crazy Family Road Trip 89

21 The Last Week of Summer: The Final Frontier 93

SECTION THREE: FALL

22 Your Babysitter Is Back in Session! Get the Kids Back to School so You Can Get Back to Life 99

23 The Neighborhood Carpool: Moms Do the Math 104

24 Braving the Bus Stop: A Field Guide for Anxious Moms 107

25 It's the Fall Harvest: Get Ready to Pick a Crap-Load of Apples! 111

26 Making a Healthy School Lunch Every Day: Never Gonna Happen. Don't Even Bother. 114

27 Don't Ask, Don't Tell: Speaking in Code When You Meet the Teachers 118

28 Who Ruined Halloween? Pretty Much Motherf*%king Everyone! 121

29 Nothing Is Funny at 4:30 a.m.: Coping with the End of Daylight Saving Time 124

30 Miserable Bitches Unite!: The Annual PTO Fundraiser 128

31 The Thanksgiving Holiday: Who's Up for Chinese Takeout? 133

32 Five Good Reasons Not to Chaperone Your Child's Field Trip 136

33 Five Good Reasons to Chaperone Your Child's Field Trip 138

SECTION FOUR: WINTER

34 Cold and Flu Season: Tired Old Wives' Tales for Tired Old Wives 141

35 The Solstice Sucks! A Winter Survival Quiz 145

36 Early Release (a.k.a. Extra Torture): Fighting Back Against Two-Hour School Days 148

37 Holiday Tipping: Handing Out Money for Baby Jesus 152

38 How to Make a Holiday Card That Isn't Ugly, Obscene, or Otherwise Inappropriate 158

39 New Year's Resolutions for Moms Who Can (Maybe) Do a Little Bit Better 161

40 Cabin Fever Is Real: What to Do If It Happens to You 165

41 If You Can Survive February, You Can Survive Anything. Even Valentine's Day. 169

Afterword 174

Acknowledgments 175

INTRODUCTION

Motherhood Is a Multi-Seasonal Affliction

It's one of those awkward life moments.

There you are, standing outside the kindergarten door with the other parents, waving goodbye to your kids. As the children disappear into the building with their turtle-shell backpacks, you suddenly find yourself sucked into a black hole of playground-based mommy nostalgia. Awwwww. They're so cute... They're so big... I can't believe it's already spring... All those baby years... are they really ***over***? SNIFF.

Your eyes are watery too. *Damn tree pollen.* But you play along because, really, do these sweet, sniffling gals need to know you're not on their sentimental wavelength? You aren't sad. You aren't emotionally overwhelmed. Secretly, in fact, you are overjoyed. Those baby years are over?... YIPPEEEEE!

You don't cheer out loud, of course. Not until you get back to the car and roll up the windows, at which point you can howl like a drunken sailor, fresh off the boat for Fleet Week. But why shouldn't dropping off your kids with another responsible adult—anywhere, really—be a moment to celebrate? Let's review some basic facts. Who managed to keep them alive during the toddler years, when they were hoisting themselves onto the hot stove to "help" you cook? You did. Who paid daycare professionals all that money to read them tactile books? You did. Who lost all that sleep when they had rotavirus and had to be rushed to the bathroom every twenty minutes with the runs? Your spouse did that. C'mon. Gross.

But no matter how many kids you have, how many hours you work, or how many mornings you feigned sleep until your husband got up to make them breakfast, the point is the same. Dry those fake pollen tears, Mom. You earned this shit!

Besides, you won't be cheering in your car for long. Allergies come and go with barometric pressure, but parenting is a year-round condition. As your kids go through the school year, you confront new challenges every day. You worry they won't make the right friends, get a spot on the right soccer team, or find their way into the right bathroom, whatever that means in this day and age. The good thing about school is that it has *teachers*. The whole reason these people are able to fulfill their lifelong dream of teaching kids how to find the "right" bathroom is that you're dumping kids off—100 percent alive, by the way—at the tender age of five. Even so, school isn't quite the mommy vacation it's cracked up to be. The kid still expects you to pitch in with folders. Teachers offer an obscene number of opportunities for parental involvement. And if school makes kids smarter, it also makes them hip to your tricks. By the time they hit second grade, you can no longer tell them that homemade cupcakes are a pretend food. Thanks, Cupcake Mom.

As the kids grow and the seasons change—whether it's soccer season, camping season, apple picking season, or cold and flu season—you still need guidance on important issues. Most of all, you need helpful shortcuts and self-serving rationales. There's a time and a place for sentimental parenting. But school drop-off is not that time and place, and neither is this book.

SECTION ONE

SPRING

* CHAPTER 1 *

Finding Your Lost Kids and Other Practical Spring Break Advice

If you are looking for advice about how to plan a *flawless* vacation with your kids, the Internet is your spring break G-spot. The World Wide Web is packed with **superIFFIC** ideas about the **perfect** towns to visit, the **best** places to eat with kids, and the **hottest** apps for jumping lines at the amusement park. Like most exciting things on the Internet, however, these ideas are also dirty fantasies. There's no such thing as a vacation with kids, and everyone knows that.

But even if you call it "a trip," the fact remains that perfect trips with kids are like vaginal orgasms: Good luck with that. Wouldn't spring break travel be easier if we got advice that was less like zesty Internet porn and more like the sex life of a middle-aged married couple? The theme of *that* spring break trip would be founded on three simple ideas: Lower your expectations. Minimize the surprises. Manage the dysfunction.

PROJECTILE VOMIT IN THE RENTAL CAR

Maybe it was a GI thing he picked up on the plane. Maybe she was playing a video game when the mountain road got unexpectedly curvy. Maybe he was enjoying a box of Whoppers when he discovered that a movie theater–size box of sugarcoated malt balls do not, in fact, go down like water.

It's not their fault. Actually, it's your fault. Before kids blow chunks, they almost always try to warn you. They grunt. They groan. They complain of a tummy problem, prompting you to instruct them, "Open a window." Real talk, parents. Fresh air? If fresh air cured vomiting, hospitals would have crank-open windows and the Ebola virus wouldn't be that big of a deal. Telling your carsick kids to open the window is roughly as effective as telling them to drink curdled chocolate milk and stare at the hood ornament.

So there you are—speeding to a Mexican airport that you just realized is in a different time zone—when one of the twins yaks onto his lap, his brother's lap, the back of your head, and the entire backseat. Why? Because kids never puke up a tiny bit. They puke up, like, two gallons. They puke up *way* more by volume than they have actually eaten in weeks, if not months. For reasons unexplained in the Bible, their puke flies out like Satan's spew.

How to fix it. The smell of puke is contagious, so you need to triage this shit. First, slam on the brakes, jump out of the car, and open the puke-side door. Next, strip the clothes off everyone who isn't already naked. Now open your husband's luggage and pull out all the large, absorbent undershirts you can find, unless you stole some towels from the hotel; don't waste time worrying about ethics—the hotel doesn't want them back now anyway.

After heavy wiping, take hand sanitizer or a water bottle and dump liquid all over the seats and your kids. Dry the seats with dirty socks, underwear, and any stuffed animals your kids may have won at local carnivals. Those toys are probably made out of toxic waste, anyway, and should be buried. When you can't do any more, find a nearby trash can. If there's no trash can nearby, leave the entire pile of puke-soaked fabric by the side of the road. Sorry, volunteer cleanup crew. But this is no time to be a good citizen.

LOST CHILDREN

The second most common spring break experience is the temporary misplacing of one's children. This one is not your fault. What are you gonna do—walk your kid on a leash? If kids were meant to be tethered like farm animals, they would sleep outside in the barn like you asked, without complaint. The problem with unleashing them is that when kids get lost, they go *invisible*. They disappear like magical wizards. That is because kids have no sense of direction. Or anything else, for that matter. They wander off like airheads with no memory and no plan for the future. And since they are roughly half the size of regular people—and 98 percent of them are wearing T-shirts—they can't be easily spotted in a crowd.

How to fix it. For the first five minutes, DON'T PANIC. Your child hasn't drowned in the fake waterpark river or been abducted by a serial killer. When kids go MIA, they're almost always doing something stupid, like hiding inside the whale belly at the playground or standing in front of a store window, staring at the flashing LED lights on a plastic replica of the Statue of Liberty. Spend a few minutes calmly looking around. He'll probably see you and charge over, scratching his head.

After five to ten minutes, you may instinctively start checking your phone to see whether your child has called you. Don't bother, Ma Bell. If your child is under ten—or is particularly bad at listening, even for a boy—he forgot every digit of your phone number the second you told him. He also forgot to ask a trustworthy adult for help, because to kids, *trustworthy* is a meaningless descriptor. To kids, all adults look the exact same amount of creepy and weird. Besides, none of this matters. The moment your kid realized he was lost in the Mall of America, he stopped short in the middle of the walkway and began bawling his eyes out, which is the official kid way to "ask a trustworthy adult for help." And it totally works. Within seconds, a nice mommy—

paranoid that the mall is full of predators, and possibly correct—will take your kid to the security booth.

If ten to fifteen minutes have gone by and you've checked the general area, your phone, and the security booth to no avail: PANIC! Start running through the mall and screaming out your child's name at the top of your lungs. JUNIOR! JUNIOR! OH MY GOD, I CAN'T FIND JUNIOR! Your goal should be to interrupt whatever everyone is doing so that they prioritize your lost child over their pre-shopping pretzel dogs. You may feel bad when Junior saunters out of the bathroom, wiping his hands on his pants. (But sidebar, low talkers: If you can't even *imagine* yelling that loud in a mall, because you're afraid people will get mad and/or think you're crazy, then, by all means, keep quiet. Being reunited with your child is definitely not worth embarrassing yourself in front of a bunch of strangers. It will probably work out.)

FAMILY VACATIONS INVOLVING CULTURE, EDUCATION, OR PERSONAL IMPROVEMENT

You may think you're being a good parent by forcing your kids to learn something on vacation. Maybe your college friend runs a travel agency that specializes in eco-holidays, and for the same price as a trip to Disney, your whole family can sleep in a Canadian yurt and forage for edible weeds. You think this sounds almost as fabulous as the trip your colleague took to China, when she hiked alongside the Great Wall. Think your kids will love that? Wake up, Chairman Mao. You're taking your kids away for spring break, not cultural reprogramming. If people liked being sent away to the Chinese countryside to improve themselves, China wouldn't be making all our iPhones now. Here are a few reasons why kids and culture don't mix.

Kids don't like to walk. Or listen. Or stand. They can run ten miles in a soccer game, swim a thousand meters at practice, and dance under a disco ball for hours wearing a polyester hot dog costume. But tell them you're going hiking—for no other reason than peace of mind—and their bodies go limp. Most kids would rather jog on a treadmill with a thyroid disorder than spend the morning in an art museum shuffling slowly through galleries and talking about the Renaissance. Unless you and your partner want to get extra buff carrying the kids piggyback alongside the Great Wall, cancel the trip.

You can't make butter noodles in a yurt. Even if your kids learn how to trap rabbits in Canada, they won't eat any rabbit. In fact, none of the things you can cook in a yurt are on the carbo-loaded white-food list. Yurts may be an extreme example, but it really doesn't matter where you go. Take them to Nashville for barbecue, and they'll scream for the frozen chicken tenders they get at their local suburban roller rink. Take them to Spain because their favorite food is ham, and they will suddenly become vegetarian. If you need a foodie experience, order tapas on date night.

Kids are better suited to fake adventure than real adventure. Remember when you missed that flight in Mexico and you had to stay overnight in an airport hotel? That was *so* hard. But not as hard as when your kid vomits inside the Great Pyramid, and it's 130 degrees, and you have to recon-crawl back through the narrow tunnel past dozens of angry sightseers. Remember the neon-blue diarrhea she got at Disneyland? That will seem like nothing when she gets bitten by a poisonous snake in the Amazon and you have to drive a hundred miles to the nearest shaman. You want to teach her about the environmental perils of monocultural farming? Buy a book about the rainforest ecosystem and read it to her on a first-world beach. She'll have plenty of time to risk her life when she's a moronic teenager.

Reminder! Excessive sun exposure can lead to skin cancer. More important, if your kids get burned on their first day at the beach, you'll have to stay inside with them all week long. You didn't travel three thousand miles to take a *staycation*. Use sunscreen!

Why Moms Should Boycott the Word *Staycation*

1. The bank bailout, bitches. Staycation has become especially popular since 2008. There's a good reason for that, and it's not that President Obama is a secret Muslim. You know a word's a problem when you can trace it back to an economic depression.

2. French bullshit. Staycation is a portmanteau, which is a fancy French word for "a combination." But defining it in French doesn't make it any better. In fact, a more accurate French phrase might be, *c'est des conneries*, which roughly translates to "this is fucking bullshit."

3. Not an actual fucking vacation. Moms who have taken a staycation know the truth. You are either taking a vacation or you are staying home. One of them involves a change of scenery, rest, better weather, and/or fun sightseeing. The other involves catching up on household chores, letting your kids watch extra TV, and maybe sneaking in a nap before dinner. Don't lose perspective on what you truly deserve: a vacation.

4. Other stupid words. For purposes of comparison, here are some other portmanteau terms that have either already become obsolete, or should.

* Bennifer
* newscast
* frenemies
* Tofurky
* Reaganomics
* affluenza
* feminazi
* jeggings

✻ CHAPTER 2 ✻

The Coolest Birthday Party Ideas Ever for Moms Who Really, *Really* Love Their Kids!

Are you one of those moms who really, *really* love their kids? If not, skip this chapter and check back in at chapter 68: "Moms Who Love Their Kids, but Not Enough to Give Them Everything They Want." If you *are* one of those then you know what it means to throw your kids the coolest birthday party ever. You've done it every year since your princess was five and you made the hideously embarrassing mistake of inviting three friends over for a sweet little tea party in the backyard. You heard about it. All. Day.

"You don't have a deluxe Blast Zone bouncy castle?!"

"Where is the crafting table for children on the visual-learning spectrum?!"

"What about the boys? Aren't there BOYS in the class?!"

"Were those gummy worms made with gelatin, cuz we are fair-trade vegans?!"

And those were just the moms!

After that debacle, you figured out that the only people who have small house parties for children these days are Europeans and art professors. Moms who *really* love their kids know what kid birthday parties today are *really* about.

AT LEAST 35 KIDS, IF NOT 100!

Sometime between 1992 and 2003, moms who really love their kids raised the birthday attendance bar. They started inviting the entire class to every single party. Not only was this idea supremely fun and prohibitively expensive, but also, once the precedent was set, people who refused to do it looked like total assholes. It doesn't matter if your kid was traumatized by the class bully. The bully is invited to the party too. Of course she is. The bully LOVES Morty the Magician. So get over to the grocery store, Mom. The whole class needs lunch, and they all hate your food!

ATHLETIC FACILITIES!

Once the bar was raised, all hell broke loose. Almost nobody has a home big enough to accommodate a bunch of kids who don't even like each other. How do you entertain an entire class? By outsourcing the party to an off-site fun place! It used to be cool to decorate a cupcake and take a few whacks at a piñata. Now, you have to reserve an indoor play space where all the "friends" can whack a piñata, THEN choose between four different sports, tumbling equipment, trampolines, and a sunken ball pit. Those on a tighter budget can try a gymnasium. These places keep costs down by literally *never* cleaning their equipment. If this all seems like too much to do, consider hiring an event planner. Someone who is professionally trained to plan a wedding can put together a birthday party that today's schoolchildren *just might* enjoy.

BIRTHDAY THRONES!

What is the point of treating your children like royalty if they can't sit their spoiled asses on an *actual* throne? Thrones aren't a new thing, but in today's birthday landscape, they're totally *de rigueur*. Though the birthday kid doesn't have to wear a crown, it's imperative that his friends sit around him on the floor like submissive plebian manservants. If your birthday boy-king doesn't get a special seat from which to summon his gifts, fire the event planner. Because that is bullshit. Kids sit in regular, ignoble chairs every other day of the year. They don't need to be discriminated against on their *special* day.

BIRTHDAYPALOOZA!

Another best practice is to extend the celebration for as long as possible. Invite kids over for two hours? Who can learn how to ride a bucking bronco in that time frame? Make clear in the Evite that parents should send pajamas with their children's riding crops. A sleepover dude-ranch party will be a little extra work because you'll have to pack s'mores for thirty-five. But as with Burning Man, a kid's birthday party is only radically inclusive if you sleep with dirty strangers in a pup tent. If that sounds tiring, or communicable, just remember: You're only going to be able to host these extravagant parties for about ten more years before it's time to start funding their cocaine addiction.

LOCATION, LOCATION, LOCATION!

If you really want to raise the roof (and your mortgage), take the mini-mes on a birthday junket. It's not just celebrities and selfish people who force everyone to fly to Aruba for not-their-own vacation. Can't fly the whole fourth-grade class to Aruba? OK, cheapskate. Then Las Vegas it is! Children aren't allowed to gamble or hire escorts there... yet. But there's so much for kids to do in a city built on greed, hedonism, and axis-2 psychological problems. Ferris wheels! Zip lines! Volcanoes! Circuses! Go-karts! Ice skating! Pick your cultural poison—Las Vegas has it all.

> ***Reminder!*** With a remote desert climate that's 100 percent ill-suited for human overpopulation, Las Vegas sends the best birthday message ever, from a mom who really, *really* loves her kid. Screw everyone else on the planet. It's ALL ABOUT YOU.

✻ CHAPTER 3 ✻

Beat Your Rugs, Not Your Relatives: Spring-Cleaning Your Way to Personal Happiness

A few generations ago, people did something called "spring cleaning," an annual family ritual that involved picking up everything—comforters, carpets, mattresses, curtains—and moving them outside to give them a beat down. Were people especially dirty back then? Obviously, yes. But they couldn't help being scummy. They were cooped up all winter with wood fireplaces, farm animals, home-cooked meals, gunpowder, sheepdogs, and fleas. Come the warmer weather, those dirtbags must have been desperate to beat the crap out of their household furnishings.

We don't spring-clean this way in the twenty-first century. For one thing, spring cleaning isn't a family affair anymore. Kids today can't devote an entire day to chores; they're way too busy with playdates. Also, we have vacuums now. And electric dryers, natural-gas fireplaces, fast-food restaurants, microwaves, chlorine bleach, and sinus medication. Because of that technology-driven hyper-cleanliness, our immune systems are shutting down, and we're all dying of superbugs. Thanks, Benjamin Franklin.

There are people who still choose to do the big annual cleaning for *catharsis*. Cleaning is a good metaphor for emotional purging and purification. But then, why stop at metaphor? How about if we *actually* took our negative feelings out on the annoying, dysfunctional objects/people we live with?

BEAT THE RUG FROM THE GUEST ROOM, OR WHEREVER YOU PUT YOUR MOTHER-IN-LAW WHEN SHE COMES TO VISIT/COMPLAIN.

Every holiday, you drive several hours to her house so you can sleep on a pullout couch of nails. You tolerate this because your husband insists his mother has delicate feelings. Her visits, on the other hand, are a semi-annual reenactment of "The Princess and the Pea"—in reverse. You clean that guest room for hours. You wash the bedding. You vacuum. You cut fresh flowers. You stack up several folded towels and washcloths. And still, she finds something intolerable about it every time. The facial soap gave her a rash. The room is too stuffy. There must be a stray dog hair on the carpet that is making her sneeze. Wildflowers are THE WORST.

You know what you have to do, Mom. You have to spring-clean the shit out of this problem. First, have your husband remove the area rug and hang it outside. Next, get an old-fashioned metal rug beater—the kind that looks like a cross between a heavy-cream whisk and a canoe paddle—and visualize your mother-in-law standing on it, complaining. Every time you think about her fragile feelings, whack the rug as hard as you can. Take that sisal bitch down, girl! You can't remove every miscellaneous speck of dust, hair, soap, and mold. But you can feel a LOT better trying.

STRETCH THE DRAPES IN THE LIVING ROOM.

Your drapes look like they used to be an outdoor rug. That's because your kids like to smear their hands on them right after they've applied sunscreen and eaten chocolate chip cookies. But the kids are by no means the only problem here. Last year, after the cats chased a mouse into the curtains, your dad—fancying himself an amateur exterminator—took several swings at it with a dirty broom. Now the drapes are smeared with chocolate, zinc oxide, mouse droppings, *and* oil from the floor of the garage.

The drapes need to be washed. But because they're made of heavy fabrics, they also need to be *stretched.*

This is your chance to practice some old-school corporal punishment, just like the British did with old Guy Fawkes. It's torture time, daddy! Stretch that fabric apart until the drapes/your dad is ready to concede that dirty brooms don't belong inside the house. You do love the guy. More important, he's too big to push over and put in a half nelson. But it's high time for someone to acknowledge that he'll never be handy. Torture the drapes until you can almost hear them screaming for mercy: "I'm no Tim Allen!"

PUT WINTER CLOTHES IN A SEASONAL TIME-OUT.

Kids are constantly being rude and disrespectful. They tell us we're weird and roll their eyes if we express an authentic emotion in front of their friends. Well, guess who's in charge of rotating your clothing, meanies? Yes, it's the weepy fatso with the wrinkly lips! Not only does she get to decide what stays or goes, but she's also free to verbally abuse your wardrobe. Remember that day in February when your kid played a bad hockey game and had the audacity to tell you that *you* were bad luck? That hockey jersey is going down. (Up, actually. Into the attic.) Then there was the time you told your other kid to finish her math homework, but she insisted on going ice-skating. This is your moment to say "I told you so." But don't bother saying it to *her*. She won't listen anyway. Just take it out on her favorite fuzzy fleece leggings. Squish that shit into a tiny ball and banish it to the back of the drawer. Then give it the finger. Skate on this, ice pants!

GET RID OF OLD APPLIANCES YOU NEVER USE, ESPECIALLY IF YOUR YOUNGER BROTHER WANTS ANY OF THEM.

Recycling is good eco-behavior. The thing is, your brother wasn't too kind last summer when poor little Snickers got blocked. Catheterizing a dog is *too expensive*, he said. Little bro—biased against dogs ever since a pit bull bit off part of his cheek—offered to put Snickers out of his misery by snapping his neck and burying him in the backyard. You still have nightmares. Does broham *really* need that juicer? If you gave him your old wok, would he start eating some healthy meals? Hmmm. Maybe. Or maybe he'll just develop heart disease from his unhealthy diet and end up having his chest sawed open for quadruple bypass surgery. Human life. *So expensive*. Put the appliances and your brother out of their misery and dump them in the motherfucking garbage.

CLEAN THE WINDOWS AND SCREENS.

Clean the windows? Yourself? Hell, no. Hire someone to do this! Your husband told you that window cleaning wasn't "in the spring budget." But baseball season has already started, and your husband hasn't gotten it done, and you're getting tired of looking at the backyard through a layer of bird shit. Get a personal recommendation for a window company. If possible, find one that employs hot young men. Like graduate students. Or baseball coaches. Nothing says *fuck baseball season* like staring out at the naked torso of Adonis as he stands on a ladder, soaping up your bedroom window. If your husband gets mad at you for gawking, all the better. Maybe next spring, he'll decide to put that pitching arm on ice for a few days, and help with the cleaning. Cha-ching.

> ***Reminder!*** An effective way to get rid of those old toys your kids are sentimentally attached to is to "disappear" them behind furniture. By the time you pull out the dresser to vacuum behind it next spring, the kids won't care about the stuff anymore. Suck it, toys.

✻ **CHAPTER 4** ✻

Matzo Balls, Lambs, and Locusts, Oh My! Whatever You Do This Holiday Season, Don't Get on the Neighborhood Listserv

A lot of people believe that playing violent video games has a negative effect on behavior. With all the scientific research devoted to kids and gaming, it seems odd that nobody has bothered to study the behavior of moms who participate in a neighborhood Listserv.

Moms often join these groups for good reasons. One person has bunk beds to sell. Another needs a hotel recommendation. The old woman on the corner started a little free library and people are stealing the books. This thievery upsets her until someone points out that the criminals probably need the books more than anyone. Bleeding-heart generosity wins. Crisis averted.

The *problem* with the neighborhood Listserv is that, eventually, the bunk beds and free library will give way to a more controversial topic. Reasonable people will disagree. Feelings will be hurt. This is especially true around the holidays, when Sh*tty Moms—from all perspectives and walks of life—come together to drive one another absolutely fucking nuts.

ALTERNATIVE-FOOD MOM

While every mom in the world gets stressed around holidays, Alternative-Food Mom is MORE STRESSED than everyone else. That's because she has to make all the traditional foods with nontraditional ingredients. She's so unconventional that she barely has time to post this question: *Anyone know where I can get some gluten-free KFP cereal around here?* She definitely doesn't have time to explain her high maintenance food requirements to "traditional eaters." But she'll do it anyway. *I'm staying gluten-free for Lent. If I don't use sweet potato flour, we will all be doubled over on the floor for the Resurrection!* After reading her missive on fair-trade organic gluten-free ethnic food, everyone else in the neighborhood feels ignorant, cheap, and bloated.

HOLIDAY-DIETING MOM

Most of us gain weight over holidays because of some combination of stress and butter. Not Holiday-Dieting Mom! She uses the religious dietary restrictions as an excuse to stop eating. Holiday-Dieting Mom has a lot of facts at her disposal, particularly about calories. *Hey, everyone—there's a gluten-free matzo now. I don't eat it. It's obnoxiously expensive, and also, why bother? Matzo is already low-carb. Passover got my people out of Egypt, and it's getting me ready for swimsuit season!* Holiday-Dieting Mom can be a touch insensitive. Like when she announces to the group, "I wish I had celiac disease so I couldn't sneak bread!" Or "I'm giving up dessert for Lent, so I can be skinnier than my sister, who is diabetic." Six long weeks with nothing for dinner but red wine. How will she do it?! Tune in to the Anorexia Holiday Listserv to find out.

ANGRY-SHOPPER MOM

Over the holidays, grocery store aisles are crowded, carts are overstuffed, and stock is low. Nobody is more aggravated about this than Angry-Shopper Mom. She insists on serving the same meal every year and if the grocery store can't accommodate her, she'll take them down. *The price per pound for lamb this year was outrageous, they were almost out of red potatoes, and their cabbage looked like shriveled human heads!* While she's pretty sure the deli guy had his thumb on the scale, she's not half as outraged as the mom who needed Passover sardines and accidentally picked up regular sardines because they were stocked in the wrong place. She'll take them back to the store to exchange them. But first, she needs to tell everyone about the store's transgression. What if she hadn't noticed? What if she had served them? What if Nanna had actually put one in her MOUTH? The consequences are *dire*, and the venting is *endless*.

STICKLER-FOR-DETAILS MOM

If this woman were British, you'd call her a scold. In America, we have a different word for her. She's that pain in the ass who's superficially nice but talks with a clenched jaw, and you can hear it in her writing every time she weighs in. Which is often. *Dear neighbors: You may wish to know that lamb meat is not necessarily the meat of baby sheep. Like mutton, it happens to be the correct term for the meat of adult sheep. Thank you.* Sometimes, Stickler-for-Details Mom doesn't raise actual topics but, instead, focuses on the process. *Please stick to matters relevant to our entire community. Thank you.* No, Stickler Mom, thank *you.*

RANDOM-ACTIVIST MOM

This mom doesn't really hear your anxiety about holiday shopping. Because whatever you said—blah, blah, blah—reminded her of a political issue she feels strongly about. *Folks: I don't know about cereal or sheep meat. But I did read an article recently about the newly protected status of sardines. How about tuna fish this holiday season?* Random-Activist Mom is a close cousin of Stickler-for-Details Mom. Indeed, they share a common goal: taking people down with a bounty of unsolicited and judgmental suggestions. *Let's all try to be better stewards of the earth, OK?*

OVERLY POSITIVE MOM

Sometimes, when people get irrationally upset, other people should probably just stay out of it. Wait until the storm passes. But because they're too positive to shut the fuck up, they instead make it worse. With the Listserv equivalent of "turn that frown upside down," Overly Positive Mom will remind everyone not to be angry and critical and judgmental, because *really, ladies, Passover and Easter should focus on happiness, gratitude, and fun!* And then, as the self-appointed spiritual leader of the Listserv, she'll sign off with an interdenominational non-saying. *Namaste, happy Ramadan, save the sardines, and God bless America!*

COMICALLY OVERWHELMED MOM

She's not so much overwhelmed as she's a caricature of someone who is overwhelmed. *Did someone just say the holidays are about happiness? Thank you for that respectful blessing, but what the HELL are you talking about?* Comically Overwhelmed Mom cleans the whole house, top to bottom. Unlike Overly Positive Mom, however, she doesn't let her personal beliefs get in the way of kvetching. On Easter: *Why do I have to plan an Easter egg hunt? Why the fuck would a bunny hide chicken eggs for children?* On Passover: *Not only is the actual meal the most boring thing EVER, but after eating nothing but matzo for a week, my kids are just beyond constipated. They can't poop at all!* When Alternative-Food Mom talks about gluten-free matzo, Comically Overwhelmed Mom responds with a humorous request for high-fiber matzo. If she didn't laugh, she would cry.

TALKS-ONLY-ABOUT-CATS MOM

This mom doesn't have human children. Her cats are enough for her. At holiday time, though—when her cats typically forget to give her anything—she gets a little lonely and spends extra time on the Listserv. And naturally, the only thing she ever wants to discuss is the problem of outdoor cats. If someone asks where to buy outdoor icicle lights, cat mom will segue to the hyper-dominant ginger tomcat that visits her yard every day. *Wonder if anyone else is struggling with his unannounced and most unwelcome visits?* Talks-Only-About-Cats Mom doesn't want to throw her dirty laundry into the "cloud" (she uses quotation marks like it's a made-up thing), but the outdoor-cat problem has frayed her nerves. Both she *and her cat* started taking anxiety medication in order to cope.

DRUNK, FEISTY MOM

This mom is a contrarian by nature, who only logs on late at night when she's already had a few cocktails. She doesn't hate alternative diets, or holidays, or indoor cats. But when she reads all the comments together, she *does* want everyone to shut the fuck up. How does she communicate this? First she claims to have an outdoor tomcat that eats nothing but kosher-for-Passover sardines and baby sheep. Then she tells everyone that she's dating the local butcher, who's *really good with his thumbs.* Before logging off, she announces to everyone that her house is completely ready for the holiday, her children are pooping regularly, and she's never been skinnier in her entire life. HAPPY HOLIDAYS, BITCHES! SEND.

Reminder! Listservs are the leading cause of reply-all disasters. If Liposuction Mom posts about her latest surgery, and you mock her in a "private" email to your husband, there's a good chance it wasn't private after all. Just apologize, avoid her at the grocery store, and never, ever log on again.

✻ CHAPTER 5 ✻

Mean Girls Yoga: Signs Your Spring Exercise Regimen Isn't Right for You

You've heard the nightmarish spiel. Maybe you first heard it following your fortieth birthday, when you went in for an annual physical and the nurse made you step on the electronic scale. *Whoa*, you thought, wishing you'd taken off more jewelry, *that is an accurate fucking machine. You know*, the evil nurse pointed out, *every year over forty, if you don't decrease the amount you eat, you will gain a pound. Whatever*, you thought, yanking on a chin whisker. *I've got this. I can totally give up cheesecake.*

With the benefit of time, however, you accept that you need to turn this around. You fucking love cheesecake, so you're going to have to exercise. You crowd-source Facebook to find an affordable gym. Some are running spring membership specials and offer BodyPump classes that friends describe as "fun." When you sign up for a trial class, it becomes apparent that this means the instructor says the word *fun* over and over into her wireless headset while you do a hundred push-ups. By the end of class, all you want to do is drown that headset bitch in the gym hot tub.

At the height of your epic self-hatred, your unrealistically fit friend gives you a free pass to yoga. This strikes you as an excellent development. Yoga chicks are strong *and* skinny. Yoga doesn't require running. Yoga teachers are too Zen to wear headsets. But listen up, Groupon. Yoga isn't for everyone. Pull the trigger on that *drishti* too soon, and you may find yourself in a really bad position.

MILITANT MOANERS

People who do yoga for fringe spiritual reasons are different from those who exercise for cheesecake. Before you commit to the class, survey the neighborhood. Is your friend's yoga studio on the hipster side of town, where none of the women shave their armpits, all the men wear skinny jeans, and people drink water only from recycled cardboard boxes? Sure, boxed water is better. Says so right on the box: "Boxed Water Is Better." But for all you know, it was just siphoned out of a rain barrel. Also, when you put down your mat at the start of class, you notice the woman next to you is already breathing like most people moan. She's in her own world. And she's there for reasons you can't possibly understand. Stay alert.

CODED LANGUAGE/TERMINOLOGY

There's weird terminology even in normal yoga classes. The teacher will say, *We are firing up Core right now, because Yoga is about Strong Core.* But if, after a few statements like these, you realize the teacher is referring to body parts as proper nouns—*put Tailbone firmly on the floor, then ask Pelvic Bone to turn up toward Belly Button*—you may be in too deep. A pelvic bone should *never* be addressed like it's capable of answering a question. Period.

A TEACHER WHO'S LIKE REGINA FROM *MEAN GIRLS* AND/OR AN ALCOHOLIC PARENT

The best kind of yoga for a cheesecake practitioner is one that encourages relaxation. If you hear a phrase like *You're not victims BECAUSE you're weak; you're weak because you're VICTIMS,* then your class is being led by a Regina. Worse yet, he's a man. After fifteen minutes of core work, Regina reminds you to do Ujjayi breathing. Since the woman next to you is still moaning, and your inner victim is distracted, you turn to your fit friend and ask what the fuck that means. Suddenly, like a scary drunk mom, Regina appears next to you. *Stop talking! Be in your own body!* A few minutes later, he circles back to squeeze your big toe and apologize. *You're fine,* he says. *I just want you to focus.* You smile. Big toe smiles. But all you can think about is cheesecake.

ANYTHING TOO SEXUAL

People who practice yoga are generally accepting of the human form. But bodily acceptance has its limits. At the end of your core work, for example, if Regina announces, *It's time to use Props,* look around you. Make sure the moaning lady isn't masturbating with one of those scratchy rolled blankets. Then ask yourself why Regina never uses precise nouns. *Take Prop,* he yells. *Put it in between Thighs and squeeze. Squeeze it! Squeeze that hot dog as hard as you can!* You ignore the odd choice of food words, because this is intense work for Core. Core is already shaking and now, with Hot Dog squeezed by Legs, Core is starting to feel like a victim. But Regina doesn't stop. *Groin should be zinging right now,* he says. *Isn't that exciting?* Hmmm. Probably possibly no.

IT'S BASICALLY A CULT

Before the standing series, Regina lets you have a drink of water. This is the part of yoga, he says, in a shaming tone of voice, when people want to quit. But they need to push through it. Because on the other side, they will be a new person. *Yes,* you think, *I want to be a new person.* I want to be more like Regina. When I'm more like Regina, I'm going to use slogans like "victim face" and "happy place" and tell people how they need to feel. When I'm more like Regina, I'll never finish a whole sandwich. I'm going to stop eating victim food altogether and instead take in a steady diet of low-carb protein bars and—only when it really hurts—a little bit of water. Congratulations. You have just cured your addiction to cheesecake—by joining a fucking cult.

YOU BARELY ESCAPE WITHOUT SERIOUS INJURY

Ultimately, the surest sign that you have chosen wrong is that the Great Leader pushes you too hard. At Regina's command, you do Arrow Lunge. You do Straddle Thing While Awkwardly Holding Calf, and Painfully Wedged Shoulder Behind Knee. This quite possibly leads to Slight Dislocation of Spine. It is a long series, and it hurts like hell. Finally, he goes too far. Right at the end, Regina tells you to stretch your eyes. *Ocular Muscle is the most atrophied muscle in Body.* Wait. What? When he's not teaching yoga, does Regina perform LASIK surgery? Who IS this bossy bitch? Suddenly, none of it makes sense. The fog starts to lift. Toss your box of rainwater in the trash, march Legs out of the studio, and vow never to return.

Reminder! You'll be a lot more motivated to exercise this summer when the kids are home practicing gymnastics on the furniture. See ya later!

✻ CHAPTER 6 ✻

Mommy's Running Off with the Gardener: April Fools'!

Spring holidays can be hard on busy moms. Take Saint Patrick's Day and Cinco de Mayo. Since this country was built by hardworking Irish and Mexican people (among others), those holidays are a great opportunity to honor their cultures and put children in green sweaters and big hats. Viva la shamrock!

The problem for moms is that in today's drunken melting pot, adults primarily use these holidays as an excuse to leave work early and get wasted. There's nothing objectively wrong with this. When you look up *fun* in the dictionary, the first two entries are probably beer and tequila. Hardworking immigrants know how to party; the rest of you are lucky to be invited. Unless, of course, you have small children.

Getting wasted in the middle of the workweek—like micro-minis, cigarettes, and going to sleep with your makeup on—is a younger, single girl's game. It's a game for women who don't have to get up in the middle of the night to change a diaper, get up in the morning to make chocolate chip pancakes, then eat the cold pancake bits off melamine happy-face plates because they're too fucking tired to make breakfast for themselves.

Some of you are scratching your heads. Wait—aren't moms drunk all the time? Cocktails before playgroup. Chardonnay in sippy cups. We've all read the books. For moms, Go Fish is just another drinking game. *Mommy, do you have an ace? Yes, honey. Now bottoms up with the hand sanitizer. It's time for you to go to bed so Mommy can paint her face and get shitfaced for Ireland.* But, no. The sad truth is that moms don't party nearly enough.

Could we have a few belts while we pick up Legos? Sure, unless we have to drive for the carpool or help with math homework. Moms laugh about drunken playdates, but actually—even in the realm of going out and drinking too much—we're falling short. We'd like to blow off steam like all the fun, drunk, single people. But we can't. Fifth-grade math is HARD, dummies!

And that is exactly why we need to appropriate *our own holiday*: April Fools'.

MOMS ARE SICK OF GETTING PUNK'D!

Kids love to fuck with moms. They've been doing this ever since they were in utero and decided—since you weren't sleeping well anyway—to stay in there an extra fourteen days and then come out upside down. By the time they are teenagers, their funny tricks are called *lies*. They punk you by saying they're going to a movie and then they go have sex with their girlfriend. In your car. If moms are sick of playing Go Fish completely sober, they're also sick of getting punk'd. It's time WE got a day to punk THEM.

USE PUNKING TO TEACH THEM A LESSON.

Hands down, the best reason for moms to appropriate April Fools' Day is to whip kids into shape. Know how your ten-year-old never picks up her clothes (clean or dirty) off the floor, even though you've asked her three hundred times? On April Fools' Day, take all her clothes—from the floor, as well as the closet and dresser—and hide them in the storage ottoman. Tell her you got sick of picking up after her and tossed all her fave outfits in the garbage. When she starts to cry, extract a promise from her that going forward, she'll be tidier with her clothes. Or how about this: Do your kids always complain about fresh vegetables at dinner and, no matter what you make, ask for grilled cheese instead? Wait until they open those lunch bags at school and see they're packed with nothing but green smoothies. April Fools', suckers!

BE NASTY JUST BECAUSE YOU CAN.

Come to think of it, kids never need a "reason" to fuck with us. April Fools' is the perfect day to piss on their selfish parade. Do mean things *just because*. You repressed your anger when your son climbed on your bathroom vanity stool and cooked a "makeup soup" with your eye shadow. So sneak into his room, systematically dismantle every vehicle he's ever made with Legos, and throw all the pieces in the middle of the rug. When he comes in, declare with the same shit-eating grin: *I made Lego soup for you, sweetie!* You kept quiet the day your twins splashed you from the pool, even though you'd just had your hair done. Won't they find it JUST as hilarious when you take their favorite painting—the one they worked on for eight minutes and forced you to hang up in the kitchen—and splash it with tomato sauce? *Oh my goodness, splashing! So messy! April Fucking Fools'!*

MAKE UP A STORY TO JUSTIFY YOUR BEHAVIOR.

Smart kids hate April Fools' Day. Of course they do. It totally sucks to get punked. So if your kids are smart, they will question why anyone would invent a day for supposedly nice moms to act like cruel-ass bitches. Give them a believable story to explain it. A long time ago—when people still worshipped goddesses and men got their periods—a group of evil dwarves/children were tired of getting cold bagels for dinner every day. So they asked the goddesses to make women be the primary caregivers, instead of the men. Women were angered at this request because, up until that time, they'd been making a *shitload* of money playing professional sports while men got low-paying jobs in social work—and nobody ever questioned how unfair that was. But the evil dwarves cried so loudly that they got their way. To appease the women, goddesses gave them one day, April Fools' Day, to remind everyone else in the family how the human race survived. So now, children, if you don't let Mommy have her special day, the evil dwarves will come back, renegotiate the contract, and put Daddy in charge of brushing your hair and cleaning your hamster cage.

SPEAKING OF YOUR PARTNER . . .

Why should kids take all the heat? Wasn't your partner the one who went bowling with his buddies on your anniversary? Wasn't your partner the person who blithely allowed your kid to eat popcorn the day she got braces and then fell asleep on the couch, leaving you to extract the remnants with a low-flow Waterpik? Use April Fools' Day to reboot your partner's sensitivity chip. Don't be afraid to enlist the help of the kids. Hack into one of your kids' iPods and—using believable spelling errors—shoot a quick text to your partner at the bowling alley. *Daddy: U might want to come home. The basement has a brown lake in it that smells like poo, and the gardener just took off Mommy's bra.* Your partner may not be happy when s/he returns home and finds you laughing your ass off. Too bad. On April Fools' Day, Sh*tty Moms do not abide.

Reminder! If any of your children were born on April Fools' Day, postpone your antics until the next day. Those dwarves are evil, but they deserve a happy birthday.

✻ **CHAPTER 7** ✻

Moms with Girls: Psycho BFFs

As the school year winds down, and the kids finish up their final round of tests, your daughter is so happy! She has finally made some new friends. One girl in particular is always hanging around. Every night they message each other with hairstyle plans for the following day. They're even planning to sing a duet at the spring talent show, which comes as a huge surprise to you, because your daughter hates being onstage. Hmmm. Interesting. Has she been stealing her dad's lithium? Is she flirting with lesbianism? Also, if that were the case, would they spend that much time talking about their hair?

It's entirely possible that your daughter's new BFF is a psycho. Your daughter is her "friend" only in the sense that she is the emotional putty the BFF uses to fill the holes in her own psyche. Over time, friendships either deepen in respect and stability or they explode into nasty emotional messes, and someone ends up taking her shirt off on the school bus. Don't let your daughter become a middle-school Snapchat sensation. Get on top of this *now*.

EVERY KID ACTS LIKE A DICK SOMETIMES, INCLUDING YOURS.

Keeping this in mind will help you distinguish between normal and abnormal problems. If your fifth grader comes home in a bummed-out mood because her BFF kicked her out of the talent show, encourage her to express her feelings. Maybe it was a misunderstanding. Also remember that a little rejection is good for a kid. You don't want her to love people in the same way as Lennie from *Of Mice and Men,* who keeps people so close he squeezes them to death. Normal friendships have ups and downs. Plus, your kid probably did the same dickish thing to another girl, like, yesterday, when the weather was cloudier and the room had a different seating arrangement.

NOBODY WANTS TO BE THE WRONG CONJOINED TWIN.

Having said that, dickish behavior is more extreme in some children. The time to start watching things carefully is when the girls become so close/bonded they're *inseparable.* Inseparable things almost never work out. Think about conjoined twins. Stalkers. Tongues frozen on flagpoles. Wishbones. Sitting next to the same person every day at lunch is totally awesome, unless your kid turns out to be the smaller half of the broken chicken bone.

BESTIE OR BULLY?

What does that *B* in *BFF* stand for, anyway? When people say the word *bully,* you typically think of boys who steal lunch money or throw short kids in the trash can. Girls, on the other hand, have "drama." This sexist assumption isn't much better than when women were diagnosed with hysteria, and their wombs were supposedly wandering around their bodies like feral cats. Women in the nineteenth century were sometimes just bored. And girls in *every* century are sometimes just mean. Are they really planning hairstyles together, or is the BFF threatening to take away behavior points if your kid doesn't follow orders? Are they really swapping food at lunch, or is the BFF micromanaging your kid's diet because she's a budding nutritionist/anorexic? Dig a little deeper, Dr. Ruth. The BFF may have given your kid newfound confidence for performing on stage. Or she may be a Scientologist who is blackmailing your child with a terrible family secret. Destroy your sex tapes, hide your strap-on, and give your daughter permission to quit the talent show.

INSPECT THE GENE POOL.

You know how sometimes you worry because your daughter is grumpy and cynical, her resting face is an ugly frown, and she gets all these shitty qualities from you? Well, we've all got issues. But if you're worried about your daughter's bestie, make a point of meeting the parents. Track the mom down at the next school fundraiser and introduce yourself. If she has no idea who you are and doesn't look you in the eye when you talk, don't worry. That's actually the principal. The *mom* is the one stealing all the bids at the silent auction table and saying her kid deserves the top prize because she "has so many behavior points at home." She's the batty bitch pushing her way to the front of the sign-up line because she is more important and talented than everyone else. Yup, the problem's in the pool. This relationship is not likely to improve with age. Ban the BFF and help your daughter find new friends. That middle-school bus is looming large.

Reminder! A lot of batshit narcissists raise perfectly nice children. If the parents are crazy but the kid is fine, don't hold it against her. In fact, give her extra empathy. She probably doesn't get much at home.

✻ CHAPTER 8 ✻

Moms with Boys: Broken Bones

Sexism is not the only reason people overlook girl bullying. The other reason is that boys are way more obvious about it. That's because boys are more obvious about everything. And thank goodness for that. Navigating the labyrinthine underworld of prepubescent girl drama is like trying to negotiate a uranium deal with Iran. As soon as you think you've got a handle on the issues, someone lies or changes the rules or drops someone else from a group text because they're jealous of her new hoodie. It's crazy and fucking exhausting. At least *some people* on this doomed planet know how to resolve disagreements with stupid jerks by punching them in the face.

The point of this chapter is not to promote sexist stereotypes about boys' roughhousing. The point is to prepare moms for dealing with the physical injuries that will result from their boys' inevitable roughhousing. Like when he swings wildly at a baseball going fifty miles an hour in a batting cage, because that seemed like a good idea. Or when he refuses to listen when you tell him not to climb out onto a low roof at his cousin's house—because he wants to see if he can touch the ground with a hockey stick by hanging over the edge. Surprise! He fell off. And now his hand is broken. Why does this fucking shit always happen in the spring? Woman, it doesn't. It happens all year round. But it does suck. Because now, after you've driven him to school all winter long, he can't start riding his bike. What's a pissed-off/worried mom to do?

TRY ART THERAPY.

Just because baseball season is ruined doesn't mean you have to keep your little dude at home every day. Art therapy has been shown to produce excellent results with the elderly, veterans, and people suffering from PTSD. Instead of running around outside, your guy can work through his frustrations by collaging an erupting volcano. Or making a healthy papier-mâché hand. Or sketching his feelings. Does this suggestion sound completely ridiculous to you? Of course it does. Stereotypes exist for a reason.

IGNORE IT.

Kids whose parents are doctors will be familiar with this strategy. Doctor-parents, sick of listening to patients whine all day about fake chronic ailments, have no problem disregarding their children's complaints. Take a page from their playbook. Tell him that swelling is a healthy physical response. If he can get the thumb into the baseball glove, he's probably just a slow healer. Besides, the only way to know for sure is to take him to another doctor for an X-ray. That will take all morning. Hand? *Pffft*. He's lucky it's not an eye.

NATURAL CONSEQUENCES.

As parents, we're always eager to find ways to demonstrate how bad choices have bad consequences. Breaking a hand by falling off a roof is a painful way to learn that only a dumbass hangs over the edge of a roof. But it doesn't matter. This object lesson is not going to teach your son a damn thing, anyway. As soon as the cast is off—like, literally, that night, and maybe even late afternoon—he'll climb back up on the roof. And this time, he'll bring a hockey stick *and* a bungee cord. *What* natural consequences? says testosterone.

BE THANKFUL IT'S NOT SUMMER.

If your son is bouncing off the walls from missing spring baseball, be thankful it's not already summer. At which time he'd miss summer baseball, fishing camp, swim lessons, robotics team, and the Boy Scout canoe trip. He's been looking forward to that trip all year because his troop leader is a great role model, knows everything about knots, *and* listens to fun music by the Village People. You need him to go on that trip. At this juncture, you're still five weeks out from summer break. He's hyperactive, but at least he's still in school. Suck it, teachers!

Reminder! If your kids repeatedly break bones because they drink sugary soda every day instead of milk, it might be time to get them checked for osteoporosis. After you do that, give your children to loving parents who don't let them drink sugary soda every day instead of milk. You're fucking this up.

✻ CHAPTER 9 ✻

Mayday! Mayday! Mayday! Weathering the Last Month of School

For most kids, the school year ends in June. Which means that for most parents, the work year ends in May. Every year—somewhere between paying your taxes and installing the mailbox your husband got you for Mother's Day—your calendar becomes so overloaded with end-of-the-school-year celebrations that you can't even remember to do your hair in the morning. Fuck it. You don't have time to look human, anyway. You have to make an industrial-size carafe of sport tea for art gallery night, fill out the application for language immersion next year, and then run over to the bathing suit store to order swim team sweatshirts. Take some small comfort in knowing that nobody with children under the age of ten will get anything done this month. You can avoid making more serious distress calls—whether to the unemployment office, your shrink, or the neighborhood meth dealer—by following these mayday procedures.

YOU ARE THE ONLY CAPTAIN OF THIS SHIP.

If you saw that movie where Tom Hanks is in charge of a container vessel that gets hijacked by pirates, you know that ship captains don't fuck around. In times of crisis, they send everyone down to the hull, give the pirates all their cash, then get captured and thrown onto a slow-moving dinghy. Is that proper maritime protocol? No idea. But you can learn from his pirate mayhem. When the PTO sends out the schedule for Teacher Appreciation Week—which it couldn't possibly host in February, when there's nothing else on the calendar—don't get annoyed and delete the email. You *need to know* that Monday is Card Day, Tuesday is Blue Shirt Day, Wednesday is Another Day Off Day, and Thursday is make a vegan side dish for the teacher dinner. Since your daughter also has a ballet recital that day, and you have an off-site meeting for work, you need to take charge. Forward the ballet information to your husband, and tell him to save you a seat. Call your parents and tell them to bring flowers. On your way to the studio, call and have a cheese-free pizza delivered to the school. Vegans in the dinghy!

KEEP THE VESSEL ON COURSE.

Even without the pirates/teacher appreciation problem, ship captains still have a lot to do in May. You have to navigate the narrow straits that exist between the end-of-the-school-year activities and the start of summer ones. When you aren't attending the kids' final Glee Club performance, you're hiring a summer sitter. When you aren't showing up to the second-grade poetry reading that is conveniently held midmorning on a Tuesday, you're stopping by Kinko's to print a release form for computer camp. (How ironic. Really: Why don't they have email?) The problem is that if you get too close on either side—watch the Glee Club and put off the sitter interview, or interview the sitter and skip the concert—there will be disappointment, tears, and a very long summer of dirty dishes. If you aim for the middle—which means doing everything a little bit badly, but doing nothing completely badly—you might not run aground.

IF THINGS GET ESPECIALLY ROUGH, PUT ON YOUR LIFE VESTS.

OK, so you ran aground. You cleared your morning schedule to take your daughter to the pediatrician for her summer-camp physical, but the doctor's office got slammed by patients with a stomach virus. You ended up missing the managers' diversity luncheon, and now you're on the HR director's shit list. You'll have to leave your post to assess the damage. Call a friend. Or another mom in the neighborhood who you hardly know, whose kids are also going to the after-school birthday party. You need to drive back to the office and make nice with human resources. If it's really bad, lower the *big lifeboat*: your spouse. Normally hiding in the dinghy with the vegans, your partner needs to get his ass up to the poop deck. Give your spouse the basics to get through the day—where's the gift, where's the wrapping paper, where's the tape, where's the kid—and suggest some healthy options for dinner. You'll be back as soon as you can to mop up his mess.

PRIORITIZE YOUR PASSENGERS.

Remember on the *Titanic* how the rich people took all the lifeboats and the poor Irish people got locked in their rooms to drown? That was sad, and even Celine Dion couldn't make it better. But there's a lesson in that horrifying episode of class warfare that pertains to Mayday motherhood. And that is, your cat is basically Irish. Any other time of year, you could fit feline dentistry into your monthly juggling act. *Not right now.* The same goes for your weight training, your housecleaning, your Clean Parks Committee work, and your volunteer job at the retirement home. Anything that isn't directly related to your kids' finishing school and starting summer activities—so they aren't sitting at home for more than one single day—takes lower priority.

THROW SHIT OVERBOARD.

You're back on course, you have poop deck backup, and you've prioritized the kids over your cat. Still, the family boat is taking in water. Your calendar is too full. You simply can't be in three places at once. Time to get rid of the deadweight. Start with the purely social obligations. It would be nice to make caramel corn for the fifth-grade graduation party. But making caramel corn and then missing the actual graduation because your car ran out of gas might send the wrong message. Same goes for swim team. If the preseason parent information meeting is the night before the hot dog party—and you really need to get to the grocery store—the kids get hot dogs at home. Better yet, throw the hot dogs over too. Give the kids cereal and take a goddamn shower. When you get up the next morning and suddenly remember it's PTO picture day—because that couldn't fucking happen in February either—you'll be glad to look half-human.

Reminder! In parenthood, the main goal is staying afloat. After that, the main goal is getting the kids on their own damn boat. Bon voyage!

SECTION TWO

SUMMER

✻ **CHAPTER 10** ✻

School's Out. Nobody Panic!

Congratulations on successfully guiding your children through another year of learning. Not a single one of your children was seriously maimed, institutionalized, or expelled from elementary school. Now that they're home, your sweet baby pumpkins can celebrate their intact sanity and limbs by helping you with household projects, squeezing you in random acts of joy, and rolling around on the grass like puppies. All of which will take about half an hour. Until . . . 3 . . . 2 . . . 1. ***We're bored!***

Summer is a bittersweet time. Expressed as a percentage, it's approximately 70 percent bitter and 30 percent sweet. That's because your kids think unconditional love should be expressed as constant attention. They prefer entertainment to quiet learning. They prefer getting served to getting up. There is no worse feeling than knowing you're about to spend the next three months with someone who thinks American Girl dolls were invented for mothers and daughters to play *together*. You need to pack up Julie, Grace, McKenna, and a few stacks of plastic meringues, and get the fuck out of this house.

1. **The library.**
   Your first escape destination should always be the public library. Nobody in your household will be cracking a book until September. But they have story time there, which means someone else will read baby books to your kids while you nap on a bench. They also have classes in things unrelated to books. Like felt art. And Claymation. And computers. Most important, this shit is *free* and *open to*

the public. This means that if you need to leave the premises to do some grocery shopping—or a full day of work at the office—your kids can stay until the library closes at 5 p.m., 8 p.m. on Mondays.

2. **Mega-errands.**
   The only thing kids hate more than relaxing at home is going to stores where they can't buy toys. Get in the car, kids. We're going to buy birdseed! With a little careful planning—i.e., not buying toilet paper for the entire of month of May—you can drag them along on several of your most mind-numbing errands. Make them shop for shit they've always assumed came from fairies, like lightbulbs. Put gas in the car, then get the car washed and detailed. Fill the propane tank. Stop by the veterinarian's office to get your prescription dog food. Hit the hardware store—five different times—for lame shit like batteries, carpet squares, garden stakes, or Velcro tabs. Finish off the week by returning purchases that didn't quite work out, like wool socks. You think *your* lives are boring, brats? Strap yourselves in.

3. **Last-minute camps.**
   It's too late to book the kids into any cool day camps. If the public library can't babysit, how about Bible school? For a long time now, your partner has been saying that the family should find a faith community. Bible camp is the ideal compromise! For a nominal fee, your children can join a children's Bible study group led by a man named Edgar, who dropped a pile of business cards at the top of the escalator at Macy's. He conducts the school out of his own home and focuses on the Old Testament. Lunch is included. Girls eat only after the men (and goats) have finished.

4. **Stay-at-home-daddy daycare.**
When it comes to childcare, SAH dads are masters of the universe. Compared with SAH moms, they have a much more relaxed attitude about inviting their kids over to your house for playdates. Or allowing them to roam around the neighborhood until they end up—wow, again?—at your front door. Unlike moms, dads feel zero shame about their shitty parenting. They just reframe it as "giving the kids more independence," or "protecting their work time." Now that it's summer, get payback for all those woman-hours you put in babysitting his kids while he got a bike ride in. When your kids start yapping their jaws about being bored, walk them out the front door, point at a SAH dad's house, and close the door again. Takes a village, bro.

5. **Summer school.**
How is it fair that summer school is available only to kids who are struggling with academics or don't know the English language? You are a mostly regular taxpayer. Get your patriot on, and hack into the website of your school system. With a few easy keystrokes, you can re-enroll your child as a foreign-born student who needs special language instruction. If you're concerned about the possible legal or ethical implications of these actions, justify it like a full-blown narcissist: Your child's presence in that classroom will speed up learning for *everyone*. If he picks up some Tagalog or Mandarin—or a more grammatically correct version of English—even better. Now that your kid is getting some, it's truly a land of opportunity for all.

6. **Supersize the lemonade stand.**
You know how kids always want to set up a lemonade stand, and the only person who actually buys it is the local community policeman, because he needs friends? If your

kids are really that bored, maybe it's time they parlay their free-market instincts into a profitable family business. *The lemonade food truck!* Throw your kids and their Igloo containers into the back of the minivan and drive to a more populated area where people are really thirsty. Like downtown Chicago, a tollbooth on the North Texas turnpike, or almond-growing areas of California. While you listen to your favorite podcast, the kids can sell refreshing citrus beverages out of the back. After one day of this new work schedule, they will never ask you to drag your fucking dining room table to the curb again.

7. **Chores through trickery.**
It's so ironic. Kids love teaching the world to sing in perfect harmony with their lemonade, but they won't lift a finger in the house. What every mom needs at home, along with more white wine–pink Viagra spritzers, is a list of chores that kids can be tricked into doing. For example, if you tell a kid to water the garden, he'll ignore you. If you offer to let him run through a sprinkler—which happens to be positioned near a dry flowerbed—he'll dash off like Achilles to get his swimsuit. For the littler ones, have fun with magic. Say, "Hey, kids, think you can turn the toilet water blue by pouring in this special potion and stirring it around with this magic wand/toilet brush?" Use your imagination, tricksy moms.

8. **Escape the room.**
One of the hottest new trends in grown-up entertainment is the "room escape" game, where adults pay money to get locked into a room and figure out how to leave. (Sidebar, Russian political prisoners: If this isn't a first-world problem, there is literally no such thing.) But why should grown-ups have all the fun? Spend a few minutes

writing down clues that your kids will never solve. Anything related to eighties music, bipartisanship, payphones, Christopher Columbus, or authority will not be familiar to them. Lock the room and hide the key. Or, if you're really tired of listening to them complain, don't provide clues at all. Just lock them in with a TV and some snacks. Within a few minutes, they'll stop pounding on the door and just watch a movie.

9. **Join a gym with childcare.**
   So your attempt to start yoga in the springtime was a bust. Nobody needs to exercise in a hot room with vegetarians, anyway. Gyms, on the other hand, have air-conditioning. The machines are parked in front of TV screens. Your baseline level of annoyance will go down when the endorphins pump through your bloodstream. And if it turns out that you don't feel better from exercise, you can stick them in the gym daycare facility and go meet a friend for lunch. Technically speaking, gyms discourage this maneuver. But if you walk in with your kids, a duffle bag, and a BOSU ball, how the hell will they know? To ensure that your kids don't betray your clever plans for at least two hours, tell them there's ice cream for anyone who lets mommy "exercise."

10. **Make Father's Day cards.**
    Sometimes it feels like we celebrate Father's Day every day of the year—or at least every day of football season. But it turns out there is an actual date in June set aside just for appreciating Dad. Unfortunately for him, he often has to go to work during his special week and miss out on the boredom/togetherness. Let Dad know how much you miss him by having the kids make homemade Father's Day cards. Don't let your kid deprive Dad of those personalized

IOUs that moms always get. Some awesome IOU ideas: IOU a father-son golf outing; IOU a private after-work violin performance; IOU a surprise visit to your office during the day; or how about IOU an office visit every day this week?

Reminder! Your kids don't always know what they need. Are they bored, or could they be hungry? Don't worry about the obesity epidemic. Feeding them another snack will use up at least twenty minutes.

✻ CHAPTER 11 ✻

Sorting Through the Stuff Your Kids Brought Home from School, Then Throwing Most of It Away

You know that thing your kids do when they have an empty candy wrapper, or a piece of paper, or the crust of a sandwich, and—instead of walking it over to the garbage can that's four feet away—they hand it to you? Most of the time, you open your hand and grab it. That's probably because you've been taking their random garbage for so many years that you don't even notice it anymore. Plus, you might be hungry for those sandwich crusts later. Here's a fun fact: The exact same bullshit happens at school. Except there, the teachers don't have time to replicate your bad parenting habits all day. So your kid just shoves his random garbage into his desk. Where it piles up, until he brings it all home at the end of the school year.

PRESCHOOL GARBAGE HAD POTENTIAL.

Little kids think their personal creations are *amazing*. This is partly your fault for clapping when they pooped. But in preschool, your child's self-admiration was still cute. The teachers sent it all home in his backpack because it reflected new "skills." Finger painting! Nature-observation drawing! Glitter-glue blobs in egg cartons! You cherished the blob art because—even though it looked like the work of a left-brained baby chimp—you still thought your kid might be a creative genius. Better save it, in case he turns out to be the Picasso of glitter glue.

BY LATE ELEMENTARY SCHOOL, IT'S JUST GARBAGE.

By second grade, his glue blobs still looked exactly like glue blobs. Along with his poor skills, he also held on to an unrealistic faith in the nexus between garbage and genius. At no time is this misguided faith more apparent than the last day of school, when homeroom teachers hand out used paper bags to all students and instruct them to empty out their desks. Does your kid dispense of anything smashed in the back of that hoarder hutch? Of course not. Because you're not there to take it, or lavish it with undeserving praise. Instead, he dumps everything into the bag, schleps the bag home, puts it down in the front hallway, and—when you finally notice it and ask what the hell it is—insists he wants to "save it." For sure. Save the desk poop. Picasso knows best.

KNOW WHEN IT'S TIME TO TOSS.

Moms feel so bad about disappointing their children. If only we actually liked their desk poop. Listen up, Young Moms: Preschool teachers don't either. The only reason they send everything home is that all that glitter-glue shit is cluttering up *their* hallway space, which they need for wet mittens and extra diapers. Put Junior's hoarding in perspective. If he left the bag sitting in the foyer, it can't be that precious to him. So you have two options. First, you can toss the entire bag. The benefit of this approach is that some of this desk garbage may actually be perishable, so by tossing it, you'll prevent ants from colonizing the living room. The other option is to go through the bag. Do it the first chance you get, or by August 16, whichever comes first. Make sure your kid isn't home, so he can't give you any input. If you choose this option, be sure to make *only two piles.* One pile is for reusable items in good condition. The other pile is for shit that is useless, broken, and/or sloppily made. (P.S. The second pile will be much, much larger.)

Pile #1: To Be Saved

* 1 empty folder
* 1 nearly empty notebook, in good condition
* 1 old plastic bag containing $6
* 1 unopened tube of antibacterial hand gel
* 3 glue sticks
* 15 pens and pencils
* 1 empty pencil box
* 1 compass
* 1 protractor
* 4 pairs of socks
* 1 recorder
* 1 calculator
* 1 Boy Scout badge

Pile #2: To Be Tossed

* 1 blue faceless rubber hedgehog, possibly found on the playground
* 1 free paper bookmark that reads EXCELLENT in rainbow block letters
* 1 desk nametag, "decorated" with the cursive phrases "I'm awesome" and "Hey peeps"
* 1 old plastic bag containing nothing
* 1 ripped-out coloring-book page of baby seals on an iceberg, badly colored
* 8 other sloppy pictures
* 1 container of Altoids containing 3 Altoids
* 1 box of Tic Tacs containing 2 Tic Tacs
* 1 box of Tic Tacs, inside a box of Altoids, containing 1 Altoid
* 1 piece of paper, laminated, called Candy Trading Sheet, listing relative values (1 piece of gum = 2 Altoids = 3 Tic Tacs)

* 1 Santa Claus Pez dispenser, never used because nobody actually likes Pez
* 1 duct-tape coin purse, hopefully not made during school hours
* 2 index card notes that read, "Do you like me? Reply and Return," both unreturned
* 1 package of earplugs containing 1 dirty earplug
* 1 plastic Slinky, mangled
* 12 incomplete worksheets, never turned in
* 4 returned math tests, never shown to parents
* 3 Popsicle sticks covered in either glue or spit
* 1 purple plastic Easter egg
* 1 half-eaten gourmet coconut-curry chocolate bar

Reminder! Kids pine for their former desk garbage only if they can *see* it. Always bury shit at the bottom of the trash can and, just to be safe, cover it with spoiled coleslaw and used coffee grounds so they won't even look.

✻ CHAPTER 12 ✻

Suggestions for Summer Vacations #1: Riding the Rails

Summertime is all about flexibility. That's what makes it so excruciating for parents. If you have a week to spare, there are ways to "vacation" with your kids without ever having to plan a fun thing or, for that matter, actually go anywhere. You could book a flight itinerary with several connections that you'd have to be superhuman to make, for example, and spend most of the week in airports. Or better yet, are you train-curious? If you've ever thought you might like to expose the kids to an antiquated form of transportation, get a round-trip ticket for the whole family on the "airplane of yesterday."

TRAIN TRAVEL ISN'T AS BAD AS EVERYONE THINKS IT IS.
Well, it's far worse than some people think. But mostly, it's sucky in exactly the ways that you would think. The train leaves late, without explanation. It stops constantly, without announcement. It changes engines in remote places for more minutes than you can believe, and then—when it finally starts moving again—it goes backward. On the whole, train travel is a mixed bag of nuts that gets you to your destination six to forty-three times slower than an airplane, and costs a lot more money.

TRAIN TRAVEL IS IDEAL FOR ONLY FIVE KINDS OF PEOPLE—SIX, IF YOU COUNT THE AMISH.
First, you will come across a lot of **train enthusiasts**. If you find yourself talking to someone who says, "Trains are more civilized than airplanes," you're talking to a train buff. These people may

not be certifiably crazy. But their enthusiasm does rely on an outdated definition of *civilization*, which involves missing their own children's weddings because of a derailment.

Second, you will meet a lot of **ailing people**. Some are just sick in the head about the alleged safety record of airplanes. Others have a pathological aversion to cow's milk. It may be that gastrointestinal ailments are a natural topic of conversation when you're sitting with a total stranger at the breakfast table. But look out: Soy-milk guy has a captive audience, and it's you.

Third, trains are great for **old people**. Don't tell this to the train buffs, but old age is the only time in adulthood when life *actually is* about the journey. Metaphorically speaking, old people don't want to reach their final destination. And in a practical sense, they don't have to. If they get to that wedding on Tuesday—or in March of the following year—it doesn't make much of a difference.

Fourth, train travel works for **foreign people**. No need to explain that.

The final category of ideal train passenger is **children**. Kids don't mind being trapped in small seats for long periods of time. That is particularly true if they have their parents' undivided attention and/or unlimited access to movies and video games. After they've watched each of their movies three times, they can push the folding sink up and down, dangle their limbs off the bunk beds, and pull out the folding tray until it breaks. If the train is delayed, kids don't care. They don't know what day it is anyway.

IT'S GOOD TO SHOW YOUR KIDS AMERICA.

Train travel allows your kids to see America in a way that air travel doesn't. *Seeing*, of course, is the operative word, because while America is going by outside the picture window, you are trapped inside the train with your children, the retiree community, and a lot of people who can't eat yogurt. It's also true that a lot of what you see from a train is the part of America that exists along the train tracks. Like eighteen-wheelers driving on the highway that's parallel to the train tracks. Rusty train bridges. Mounds of old tires piled up next to dilapidated sheds. Burned-out shells of old VW buses. Discarded plastic bags. Discarded plastic chairs. Shredded tarps. Broken buckets. Scrap metal. Mobile homes. Next vacation, you might decide you'd rather just see an in-flight movie.

AIR TRAVEL CAN BE HARD, BUT AT LEAST IT'S TRAVEL. One thing people in the train community always say is they've gotten "fed up with air travel." They don't like getting "herded around like cattle," dealing with airport security, standing in long lines, or waiting on the tarmac during weather delays. Oh, airplane horror stories are REAL. A delayed airplane crew tells passengers to go into the airport to grab lunch and then—when the plane is suddenly cleared for takeoff—it takes off with their sleeping infant. Even on a seamless travel day, taking an airplane can be worse than a school picnic: such terrible food, so many kids. But, sorry, train buffs. Air travel remains the only way to visit another country and the only way to get to a six-day vacation destination across the country. *Staycation* may be a fake word, but *train travel* comes pretty close.

Reminder! Trains beat planes in one important way: Trains are basically warehouses of bottled water on wheels. Also, you can carry water in your suitcase. You may never get to where you're going. But when you don't get there, you will be *hydrated*.

✻ CHAPTER 13 ✻

Suggestions for Summer Vacations #2: Visiting Relatives

Except for the crazy mean ones who blow kids' college money on booze and race cars, relatives are awesome. They love you, you love them, and unless they live in your house, they are usually willing to take care of your kids when you are sick of them.

Their unconditional love/domestic separation makes grandparents, uncles, aunts, and cousins the *best people* for your kids to stay with when you want to take a real vacation. If your relatives are not robust enough to handle several consecutive days alone with your kids, however, consider *taking* them for a visit. That way, at least, they can be bored at someone else's house for a while. What could possibly go wrong?

GRANNIES CAN BE QUIRKY.

When Grandma comes to your house, she is always super helpful. She scrubs your vegetables, washes your sink, and irons your kids' clothing. Before your fastidious mom came to visit, you didn't even know you *had* an iron. But remember that if granny is tidy in your house, she'll be textbook anal in hers. She may keep it together when your boys knock over an old potted cactus in the backyard playing touch football and, right after that, take down a decorative ceramic rooster that Grandma has kept—perfectly intact—since 1962. She may tsk and roll her eyes when your youngest refuses to drink his freshly made apple juice because it "tastes like apple cider." But when your oldest belches at the dinner table, don't be surprised if she goes old-school on his ass and tells him to finish his meal with Puddles in the *actual* doghouse. Stay-at-home granny don't play.

GRANDPAS ARE JUST OLDER DADS.

Gramps is also a cool guy. The kids love his version of old-school parenting. He lets them roam around the place like feral animals. When you're out getting your hair washed, he lets the kids play in the shed with the power tools. But ask yourself: Did he really *let* them do that, or was he just watching a rerun of *Jeopardy!* and had no idea where they were? While fastidious Granny makes you tense, inattentive Grandad makes you fear for your children's lives. You'd like to say you were relieved when, at the end of the first day, the kids were ready for bed. But you really can't say that. Because Gramps—who offered to set up their sleeping space—put the air mattresses right next to an overloaded bookshelf that looks like the Leaning Tower of Pisa. The only rusty tool he doesn't have is a protective wall bracket.

LIVING THE GUEST-ROOM DREAM.

Your sister set you up in her guest room. Well, it's actually a converted home office. It's also the only room in the house that has a landline. And because she's a little bit deaf from all her years of turning tricks on construction sites, she keeps the ringer volume set to eleven. Every time the pharmacy calls (which it does fourteen times a day, because she's a hot mess), you are startled off your hide-a-bed. Also disruptive is when your brother-in-law comes in—first thing in the morning—to call the cable company. He wants to complain about another interruption in service. Does he realize the person on the other end of the phone is a robot? Unclear. She didn't marry him for his intellect. She married him for his functional power tools. But you could explain the robot thing to him. Now that you're up.

KICKING IT IN THE SUBDIVISION.

While grandparents are fun, many also live on fixed incomes. To save money, perhaps they relocated to a modestly priced place in a warm climate. Welcome to their new subdivision in Middle-of-Nowhere, Florida! It's quiet, residential, adjacent to a nature preserve, and includes membership to an adults-only golf course. For older people, this place is perfect. For parents with small kids, it might as well be the epicenter of the zombie apocalypse. There is no school playground. There is no ice-cream store or laser tag. There are no places to go at all, other than the strip mall anchored by a Kohl's, and the marsh, which may or may not have alligators. After nearly contracting tetanus from those power tools, your kids have moved on to doing *literally anything they can think of.* This includes seeing if they can fit through the doggie door, filling pitchers with cold water and doing the Ice Bucket Challenge, pushing one another around on Granny's decorative antique wheelbarrow/coffee table, and attempting to close one another inside the "guest room" hide-a-bed. Need an outing so you don't lose your mind? The marsh it is!

Reminder! Kids and grandparents are natural allies because they both have to put up with your bitching. Try to foster a close relationship between them so you can spend a few extra days away, bitching to your girlfriends.

Never Be Yourself with Your In-Laws

Nothing's better than a big family reunion. If you reunite with your *own* family of origin, you can drink a lot, laugh at your sibs, reminisce about old times, and—if he gets out of line with your daughter—threaten to rip your adopted cousin's balls off.

At the in-laws' place, you have to be more circumspect. You want to connect with everyone and catch up on their work promotions. But you need to steer clear of candor. When your brother-in-law shows up to make his famous homemade enchiladas, for example, don't comment on the canned sauce. When his wife asks everyone at the table what they're most looking forward to this summer—because she's a Zumba instructor who's UP ON PEOPLE—don't say the week your kids go to sleepaway camp. These plain speakers don't understand your cynicism. They exercise every day, instead of popping pills. They already think you're a ho for getting pregnant before your wedding, and now you got jokes?

Also, avoid getting stuck in other people's crossfire. If you find yourself sitting on the patio with Grandpa and one of your nieces tells him she's thinking of quitting her job and moving to Hawaii to buy land on a commune and live in a tiny home with her new boyfriend, Ziggy, whom she met last month at Coachella, and Grandpa looks at her like she's just killed him a little bit, don't stay put. Gramps is about to launch a lecture about how the United States won the Cold War. Spill salsa on yourself to change the subject. If that doesn't quell the tension, then make a quick run to Kohl's. They probably have a pharmacy there.

✻ CHAPTER 14 ✻

Suggestions for Summer Vacations #3: Camping

Kids like camping. This may be because they have a lot in common with Neanderthals and are comfortable in natural surroundings. To their brains, camping has it all. Dirt, noise, late nights, uncooked foods, outdoor fire, semipublic urination. The fact that kids can have all of those things—and don't have to bathe or shower for days—also makes camping an ideal way to prepare them for life in a college dorm.

Most normal moms, on the other hand, despise camping. Moms dread nothing more than driving somewhere to set up a satellite house that is even messier and less quiet than their primary home. Moms work too hard to potty train their kids to see it all slide backward in a hollowed-out tree trunk. Moms *need* cell reception. If you have to go, because your family is hot for nature, try to focus on this: As bad as camping is, it's still more pleasant than either having a baby or getting a colonoscopy. At THIS shit show, at least you can drink beer.

DON'T WORRY, IT'S NOT REALLY CAMPING.

Except for those rugged outdoorsy types who start family camping when their kids are still nursing so they develop an early immunity to deer ticks, most people don't actually camp in the "great outdoors." We camp in the not-so-great outdoors. We purchase a parking spot adjacent to a clearing of land in a manicured forest, with running water and a community outhouse. We may *tell* other people that we've gone camping when this charade unfolds. We might even take a short hike one day, to get more beer, and develop a tiny callus. But in fact, car camping has never brought a single human being closer to a spiritual awakening. You can't find yourself if you already know where you are. Which is camping space 114-D. Call this game what it really is: playing homeless.

REAL CAMPING IS DANGEROUS.

People get sick and die in nature *all the time.* You tell your friends you're going off to explore the island, but three days later—when you're eating your last wild blueberry, hallucinating a swarm of spirit banshees, and praying to Saint Michael for a rescue copter—it becomes apparent that you were never actually on an island. Real nature also has animals. Even if you *don't* get chased by a grizzly bear that buried human remains in its cave, you will stay up all night flinging metal plates at hungry raccoons. Unless you know how to fix a hole in your water canteen with chewing gum and duct tape, embrace the mantra of our old friend Buffy the vampire slayer: The main goal, always, is *staying alive.*

PEOPLE WHO THINK REAL CAMPING ISN'T DANGEROUS MIGHT BE DANGEROUS.

You know those Outward Bound fanatics who sleep alone for days in the wilderness? Have those people ever fucking seen *Deliverance*? What about *Wild*? We aren't all as macho as Cheryl Strayed, either. Here's a tip, mom-ladies: If you are out hiking with your kids and you come across a campsite that has nothing but a tent, a loaded gun, and an empty bottle of vodka, you shouldn't hang around and try to make friends. You may regret not making their acquaintance when you wake up after a long night of heavy rains to find that your head is two inches from the (new) bank of the overflowing river. But really, they're probably gone, anyway. Rednecks can seem scary in the wild, but they are smart enough to know when to hit the Motel 6. Fuck that shit. Rain camping blows.

THE MOST DANGEROUS THING ABOUT CAMPING IS YOUR OWN KIDS.

If you don't want to car camp, there are other options. Rustic cabins near taverns. Trailer parks near truck stops. Fancy beach towns with pro-squatter laws. While none of these options will allow you to commune with nature, all of them will keep YOU safer from the greatest danger of all: *your own children.* Sound overly paranoid? Try telling your kid that the river water is unsafe to drink. When he jumps in and immediately swallows the giardia equivalent of a Big Gulp, he'll spend the night puking out the door of the tent, with you on the assist. Will you survive? Maybe. Until the next day, when you discover that his expensive orthodontic retainer is still sitting in that tent-side pile of vomit. But kids don't need deadly bacteria to make your life miserable. No matter how carefully you plan the menu—portioning out Jell-O squares into ice-cube trays—you *will* run out early. Why? Because camping is hot and boring. So instead of eating the Jell-O squares, your boys will start throwing them at each other. Then they'll leave the hot dog buns open to be devoured by birds, and tip over your only canister of fresh water. Turns out, kids are just as clumsy and incompetent outdoors as they are indoors. Except out there, the stakes are so much higher.

Reminder! There is nothing wrong with pitching a tent in your backyard and calling it a camping adventure. That is especially true if you can sleep in your own bed while the kids are outside alone. Outward Bound, Sh*tty Mom–style.

✻ **CHAPTER 15** ✻

Should I Have Had *One More*? No. And That Baby Hates You.

As kids get bigger, summer (for moms) almost becomes fun again. Just a few years ago, you couldn't even have *imagined* yourself relaxing on a beach while the kids buried each other alive. You'd spend your whole day at the pool "watching them" jump off the diving board. You still have to contend with the standard summer crap salad of sunscreen, camp forms, athletic meets, and stinky backpacks full of wet towels, which kids somehow *never* get old enough to hang up. But now that they're old enough to swim, they can get their friends to watch their dumb fake tricks. And if they ask you to play with them, you can actually just say no. *I only played when you were little so you'd have good self-esteem, sweetie. Now go use it to play by yourself. Mommy's reading an article about breast implants.*

What could possibly blacken this bright spot in your parenting journey? A *baby*, of course. A cute chubby baby who sits down next to you at the pool while you're happily reading alone. He has fat rolls *everywhere*. He's gumming his mom's shoulder and tasting his little clenched fist. He's smiling at you. He's got dimples. But the worst part *by far* is his outfit: He's wearing nothing but a swim diaper and a tiny T-shirt that says FUTURE LADIES' MAN. *Yes*, you think. *That's so true.*

Cue the meaning-of-life spiral. *Why aren't my kids that bald? Why don't they do cute tricks anymore, like lifting up their arms when I say "SO BIG" in a dopey Elmo voice? Why didn't I enjoy those precious years of soft skin and toothy smiles? Oh my God... should I have had one more?!* And just like that, your sweet summer day turns into a pity party. You need to put an end to this now, sister, while you/your spouse still has time to enjoy those implants.

TELL IT TO YOUR VAGINA.

Even if you don't remember, she does. She still has PTSD from when the shoulders came out. She felt really bad for that nurse who had to clean up the spontaneous pool of pee that happened when you stood up to open the door. Look, women don't like to be treated like we're enslaved to our female organs. We know that if we get pissed off at work—even if we're a tenured doctor who's the head of the department and who oversees groundbreaking medical research—men will assume we're "just premenstrual." Like they know what "just" in that sentence even means. But we do have hormones. And babies can activate them remotely. Woman, get control of your ovaries! Your prefrontal cortex is being ambushed by your pituitary glands, and your vagina—having only just clawed her way back to 100 percent Kegel functionality—is *not* going to like it.

RENT A BABY.

If community swimming pools knew what was good for humanity, they would offer Rent-a-Baby programs. These programs would help everyone by allowing new moms to hand their blubbery babies to older moms for short, preapproved slots of time. While the new moms took a dip, grabbed a beer, or caught some badly needed shut-eye on a deck chair, the older moms could sit with the spitty blobs of cuteness and get a legal dose of baby love. The real genius of this program, though, would be the reverse handoff, when the older mom was *done*. See, older mom, you *did* enjoy those baby years of soft skin and toothy smiling. You don't fully remember it because the baby years are a long slog through eight-minute intervals of exactly five behaviors: happy, fussy, eating, sleeping, and pooping. So after you bounced your soft chubby baby on your lap for fifteen minutes, it was time for him to poop. Probably on your lap. Then you had to cover him in a towel, get up with a heavy diaper bag, and rush him to the swimming pool changing table. Three seconds after you washed your hands—one at a time while you switched him onto the other hip—your ladies' man started screaming from hunger. With Rent-a-Baby, you never have to wonder why you stopped after fifteen minutes, or at one kid.

GO OUT TO DINNER WITH A NEW MOM.

If your local pool doesn't rent babies, take matters into your own hands. Nothing clarifies the battle between the brain/vagina and the ovaries like going out in public with children and trying to get food into your own body. Go ahead, older mom, sit down. Give each of your older kids a mobile device and a kid's menu to read, *on their own*. It will definitely irritate you when they ask if the grilled cheese is "the normal kind," when they fight over the seating arrangement because one of them wants to be next to you and the other one doesn't want sun on her scalp, and when your son interrupts your conversation to ask where the bathroom is located. But when that happens, you'll give him a warning look and remind him to find the bathroom with his eyes and legs instead of with his mouth. And even as this mini-drama unfolds, you will still be able to move a fork from the plate to your mouth with 100 percent success. Your new-mom friend? She's hovering at just under 18 percent. The spit-meister is screeching in his high chair like a caged pterodactyl, and while she offers him treats in a frantic and futile effort to assuage his irrational anger, the ice cubes are melting into her only cocktail. This woman is a shell of her former self. More important, she's a shell of your current self.

TALK TO YOUR HUSBAND ABOUT IT.

If that tour through Jurassic Park didn't do the trick, kick the conversation upstairs. Husbands are mostly chill, but there are a few things they really don't like. They don't like to be micromanaged. They don't like it when they forget stuff they needed to bring somewhere, because you didn't want to micromanage. They don't like to open their briefcase at work to find the dirty socks you put in there because you were sick of micromanaging their messy pile of shit. But if there is one thing that a husband doesn't like—most of all—it's when his wife wonders out loud if his vasectomy was a "mistake." Yes, it was a simple outpatient procedure. The actual pain he experienced was roughly equal to a premenstrual headache. It was "just" surgery on his penis. But he did (finally) get it done because it was his turn to handle the birth control. And also, you promised him more sex. It's over, woman. Turn the football game back on. The vas deferens has spoken.

ASK THE PEOPLE WHO HAD MORE KIDS.

Whenever you talk to moms who have one more kid than you, they always say the same thing: *I couldn't even imagine life without her*. These people are sweet. But they are lying. Here's the thing, Octomom. Not *liking* to imagine life without your kids—because that is the mom equivalent of killing them—doesn't mean you *can't*. And in a practical sense, you already do. Every time you drag them to an older sibling's gymnastic meet and make them play underneath the bleachers, you are effectively imagining life without them. Every time you let her watch *The Hunger Games* with her older sibs—even though they're twelve, and she's four; and when *they* were four, you sat *with* them and watched *Sesame Street*—you are pretending she doesn't exist. Nobody blames you. Once the ratio of kids to parents tips over one to one, parenting becomes a game of fucking whack-a-mole. Younger sibs get whacked the most. So talk to these moms of multiples. Look into their lying eyes. Thank them for populating the world with resilient people. Then wave to your kids in the pool and return to your magazine.

CONSIDER YOUR OWN UNGRATEFUL KIDS.

Even if those moms aren't lying, they're definitely all suckers. Babies love you, mostly because they need you. But eventually, they don't. This summer, your pre-tween daughter went to sleepaway camp for the first time. You were sure it was too early. You figured she'd get scared, freak out, and send out a distress call. So you paid big bucks for a special mail system called Love Notes that allowed the camp to deliver your notes *immediately*, and then she never wrote back. She was having so much fun. She was *soooooo busy*. Don't bother letting her know how busy *you* were when you sat up all night pasting sonogram pictures into her baby book instead of sleeping. Or how busy you were the night the sitter called the theater and interrupted your favorite musical—the one with the cursing hand puppets—to say that the baby had thrown herself headfirst out of the crib. Save yourself the future heartache. Babies are cute and everything. But in just a few years, they become cruel ingrates who forget you even exist.

Reminder! If you need further convincing, look up the prospective cost of sending another kid to college. Then google "price of boob job." Comparison shopping. Just sayin'.

✻ CHAPTER 16 ✻

Go Away, Kid: How to Make Sure Your "Homesick" Kid Goes to Camp

Raising a kid is exactly like owning an iPhone. No sooner do you figure out how it works than they roll out a fucking upgrade. The same principle applies to kids and summer camp. You will, eventually, have the big kid who goes away to overnight camp and forgets about you. But before *that* upgrade happens, you first have to figure out how to deal with the kid who—after his day camp was already bought and paid for—clung to your leg like a sea barnacle and refused to go. Which was weird because, like, yesterday, he was 4 and hated you. The secret to coping with your teeny techno-overlords is remembering that—no matter how severely their operating systems are glitching—it's temporary. Like Bill Gates always says: This too shall pass. Kids have all kinds of excuses for feeling hesitant about a camp. The vast majority of them are either momentary, resolvable, or totally invalid. Here are some complaints you may encounter before the next rollout, and the tech support you need to fix them.

1. **"I'm scared."**
   Nobody likes a sissy, least of all a mom who just spent forty-five minutes trying to fit a double bass into the trunk of a Prius for strings camp and was looking forward to having a week alone so she could finally catch up on *Bloodline*. But if your kid is acting scared, it's probably not a pretext. He may be dealing with authentic fearful feelings. You know how the Inuit have lots of different words for snow? Well, you need to figure out what kind of

fear he's feeling. Start big: *Do you fear for your life?* If the answer is yes, try to figure out exactly what kind of mortal danger he believes he is in. *Do you fear that you'll be struck by lightning when they force you to play orchestral music in a thunderstorm? Do you fear that zombies are hiding behind the stand-up paddleboards, waiting to eat your brains?* After the concrete questions, move on to less acute, more amorphous versions of fear. *Are you maybe just not used to being away from home, but the counselors will be there all the time and be totally fun?* Obviously, this is a linguistic trick. By the time you get down the list from the worst-case scenario to his actual fear, it will hopefully sound funny, embarrassing, and silly. Ba-bye.

2. **"I feel sick."**
You know those emoticons in the doctor's office that are supposed to help people rate their pain, even though the worst pain face is nowhere near as bad as how women actually feel during childbirth? Channel the bad face chart. What does your kid look like? If she's about to start a three-week theater camp and her skin looks flushed and there's a tear running down one cheek, you might want to keep her home. Your convenience isn't actually worth the entire fourth-grade cast of *Beauty and the Beast* coming down with stomach flu. But if her mouth is a straight line, and her eyebrows are only slightly slanted, she's probably just nervous. Kids sometimes get stomach flurries when they're starting a new activity. To get over it, all they need is a hug and an extra trip to the bathroom. Single-session diarrhea with no fever is probably just a bad case of butterflies, and it'll stop as soon as the kids start their first game of Lap, Lap, Clap, Snap or (in her case) Toilet Paper Icebreaker.

3. **"I don't know anyone here."**
   Depending on the kid, this can be a legitimate glitch. Some people are more extroverted than others. Some of us would be perfectly happy throwing ourselves a birthday party and inviting random guests/stalkers from the Internet. We could rent a ski lodge with a family we just met on a cross-country train and, as long as they didn't have a religious aversion to coffee, vacation together for a week in Montana. Other people, being introverts, can't partake in hobbies and activities without a predetermined wingman. Because they don't make friends easily, crowds of strangers seem overwhelming and hostile. What your introvert needs to learn about the world is that the deck is stacked in the extroverts' favor. Personal success—unless you love computer science and know how to program by the age of 10—requires good social skills. Remind your kid that meeting new people can be fun and fabulous. And that if he doesn't get his shit together and go to computer camp, he will probably end up driving a middle-school bus.

4. **"It's not quite what I expected."**
   If your kid is articulating himself this eloquently after his first day at horseback riding camp, you better hope that he's somehow related by blood to the queen of England. Because if not, you've raised a self-actualized monster. *Not quite what you expected, sire? So sorry. Perhaps you expected the horses to be dressed in matching bridle plumes? Maybe you believed that, despite having never ridden a horse before, you'd be given a gilded riding crop and instructed in the art of dressage?* Your little prince doesn't like having to clean the stables, and make lanyards? Tell Prince Charles that almost nothing in life is ever quite what you expect. Parenting, for example. Part of growing up is accepting the gap between reality and

our expectations. And the reality is, he's going to camp because you've got shit to watch on Netflix.

5. **"You MADE me sign up!"**

   There are two possible scenarios at work here. The first is that she is correct. You knew you had a big deadline or business trip coming up and needed to find something that would keep her busy. Your summer sitter, bless her dumb heart, just isn't clever enough to keep her occupied all day long. So you surfed the Web until you found a camp you *thought* she'd enjoy, and you were wrong. *My bad*, you tell her, *I won't do it again*. The second and much likelier scenario is that your kid is a lying snake. Right now, she's having a tantrum in front of the dance teacher, the students, and all the other parents, including the overly passionate dance mom with the unfortunate belly shirt. Three months ago, however, your kid was screaming—also in public, by the way—that "YOU NEVER LET HER DO DANCE CAMP." Now that she's tired of dancing for one minute, or angry at you for working today, she is rewriting the life script. Don't give her this kind of creative license. *Save it for your future therapist, child, because this shit is NOT happening. Have a good time with your jazz shoes and your crocodile tears and your bad memory. I'll come back after work.*

> ***Reminder!*** If your kid does start therapy later in life, her bad memory will come back to haunt you again. She'll misconstrue every decision you made. It may be hurtful. Try to take solace in the fact that one day, her little assholes will do the exact same thing to her.

* CHAPTER 17 *

The Fourth of July for Kids: Lessons About America They Don't Teach in School

The founding fathers of our democracy may have been sexist, and racist, and not all that democratic, but they were *smart*. They set up the Constitution, a legal framework for nationhood that—with the exception of about ten key amendments—has guided this country with utter clarity for more than two hundred years. And fortunately, kids still learn a lot of this history in school. Because on the Fourth of July, we are way too busy exploding shit, and watching other people explode shit, to teach our kids about patriotism. If kids actually learn anything on the Fourth of July, it probably looks something like this.

LESSON 1: THE WILD WEST

America is known as a "free country." Historically, some areas of the country have been freer than others. The Wild West—settled by gun-toting cowboys in lawless frontier towns—is one of those areas, and its traditions have happily endured. How do we know this? Because we have history books. And also illegal fireworks. In this country, you are guaranteed the freedom to cross state lines with an older male relative at almost any time of the year, pull over to an abandoned fruit stand off the highway, and fill your van with dangerous, illegal explosives. Some people take this freedom even further by forging special fireworks "permits" in their basement or garage. The best part is that even if your family doesn't buy illegal fireworks, you can still partake in the criminally negligent social chaos. Perhaps you live in a big city where the Mafia still pays off the police to turn a blind eye to firecrackers. Or maybe your next-door neighbor has a few M-80 rockets left over from last year, that—when stored improperly and exploded spontaneously in the front yard—can rip off a human face. Yee-haw!

LESSON 2: MANIFEST DESTINY

The United States was created through expansion and settlement from coast to coast. Every year on the Fourth of July, we commemorate this history by finding ourselves a spot in a nearby park or golf course from which to watch fireworks. When people put down their sheets and blankets, they communicate an important patriotic message to everyone who comes after them: *Stay the fuck off, new immigrant.* Latecomers to the show are certainly welcome to join in the fun. But they need to do that from the downslope of the hill or underneath a bushy, overhanging tree. What should our kids take from this lesson in settlement and displacement? That if early Americans hadn't moved westward with maps and flags, the only people living on this continent now would be the people who were already living here. Don't forget to anchor your sheet with some heavy rocks, kids, so nobody can sneak up and steal your job.

LESSON 3: HOME OF THE BRAVEST

Americans are a bona fide brave people. We remind ourselves of that every time we honor our veterans, honor our soldiers, or make a joke about World War II at the expense of the French. We also remember our bravery on the Fourth of July, when parents force their children to endure a sixteen-hour death march of parades, baseball games, egg tosses, parties, cookouts, and—at the very end, long past the time they normally go to bed—an insanely loud fireworks show. What should parents do with kids who get scared, and may end up weeping out of sheer exhaustion and sensory overload? Try tossing them a couple of glow bracelets. Force feed them more pie. For the real little one, consider just leaving him at home. He may ask you to stay there too, to keep him company. Fuck that! Just send him under the bed with the dog and tell them both not to crawl out until they're ready to fight again.

LESSON 4: THE GILDED AGE

More than a hundred years ago, Theodore Roosevelt and other great reformers swept in a new era of regulation to keep Americans safe from robber barons. And we never ate shitty fast food again. The end. Thank goodness we still have the Fourth of July, then, so parents can teach their children how to be unruly and irresponsible. Because really, what legal minor needs "big brother" watching over him while he sticks an ignitable sparkler into a fire pit and waves it around over dry grass? What child needs to be reminded to clean the bug spray and sunscreen off her skin before she goes to bed? And, whatever you do on the Fourth of July, don't make homemade cupcakes with natural ingredients. In fact, the best way to beat back socialism is to buy store-bought cupcakes with artificial food dyes, sugary syrups, and processed ingredients. So this Independence Day, take out that toxic can of aerosol spray and paint stars and stripes all over your face. Do it for your country and your kids. USA! USA! USA!

Reminder! French people celebrate their independence on Bastille Day, which is July 14. Much like Americans, they enjoy military parades, music, fireworks, and traditional picnic foods like chicken liver mousse, cream puffs, champagne, and quiche.

* CHAPTER 18 *

Help! My Babysitter Sucks!

Bad babysitters are not the world's most vexing problem, but they can feel like it to a mom. Like pollution, bad sitters poison the ecosystem of your household. Like nuclear weapons, bad sitters can't be unilaterally disarmed. Because if your sitter quits and forces you to find an emergency substitute without a sufficient background check, you might hire the nanny equivalent of Vladimir Putin, who—after several glaring irregularities in the interview process—will literally never leave.

Every summer, you hope for a miracle worker. Someone who'll take away the children's iPods from time to time, teach them a few languages, keep the house stocked up on bananas, heal the dog of its compulsive scratching disorder, fix the leak in the living room ceiling, and convince your husband that having sex once a week is more than enough to keep you happily married. Well, if that magical nanny exists, she didn't apply. Maybe she already works for Ben Affleck. But if you hire a sitter for the summer who doesn't work out, just keep it in perspective, sister. There are problems, and there are *problems*.

1. **She's always texting.**
   You hired this woman to play with your kids, not stare at her phone. Does her constant texting bug your kids? Sometimes. But they're used to it. Because nobody under the age of thirty-four can do anything—with the possible exception of defecation, sex, and occasionally driving—without a mobile device in hand. Also, that's exactly how you act when *you* babysit them. Next.

2. **She can't cook.**
   Every night, you hear the same thing from your children. The only meals your sitter can make—without burning the food or burning the kids with her microwavable dishes—are mac and cheese (from a box), puppy chow, popcorn, and turkey sandwiches. The rest of the time, she takes them out for shitty fast-food burritos. Perfect. Those are also the only things your kids actually eat.

3. **She's messy.**
   You don't love how every night when you step in the door, you have to wipe crumbs off the counters, pick up dirty clothes, and put away the toys and games. You've tried teaching her how to empty the dishwasher and do the laundry. But no matter how many times you ask her, she can't reform her lazy, messy ways. Well, no wonder the kids like her. She's just like your husband!

4. **She's a little dumb.**
   The first time she called your office, she'd forgotten the garage code. The second time she called, she'd forgotten your address. She's definitely not a brain surgeon. And that's probably a good thing, because when this human dipstick lets the kid go down a slide headfirst on his skateboard, you'll be really glad the brain surgeon is on duty at the hospital instead of at your house.

5. **She sometimes falls asleep.**
   If she's an older lady, she can't help it because her husband probably snores at night. If she's a college girl, she can't help it because she's partying too much. Either way, can you really blame her? Taking care of kids is boring. That's why you went back to work, remember? Give her the Starbucks gift card you got from your co-workers and move the fuck on.

6. **She sometimes falls asleep at the pool.**
   Are there lifeguards? Then you're good. Those people are trained to save kids from drowning. If there *aren't* lifeguards, however—and sleeping beauty is expected to keep your children from drowning—then you need to draw a line in the proverbial sand. Sleeping is only permitted at the house, when the television is on duty. Meanwhile, don't worry too much. That mom who caught her sleeping and told you about it will *totally* be watching your kids.

7. **She wants more money.**
   Crappy babysitters are tolerable, unless they believe they aren't crappy. Let's say that one morning, your employee discloses that she needs more money. Even though she didn't attend college, can't drive, and curses even more than you do, she now feels that the salary she accepted when you hired her is insufficient. Have a direct conversation in which you discuss how she might earn a raise—in the future. If she insists on getting more now, spell it out in simpler terms. Three words: *Target is hiring.*

8. **She doesn't like kids.**
   Kids don't pay that much attention to what's going on around them. That's why they yell in libraries, sing on the toilet, and get lost in their own neighborhoods. When it comes to the character of babysitters, however, kids are as clairvoyant as soothsayers. They know when someone is using them as a placeholder until she can get her dream job at Chipotle. They can tell that she's an only child who hates sharing. They can see that she's not actually "busy cooking" when she refuses to play. You're not paying this woman to steal your best lines. You're paying her to keep the kids alive and, more important, to run them around so they're tired when you get home. If your kids aren't tired because the

sitter is a selfish asshole, get rid of her. The world is full of nice people with siblings who might like your kids.

9. **She is constantly late and/or calls in sick.**
   One morning early in the summer, the new sitter texts you to say that her back hurts and she can't come to work. This confuses you because your back hurts every day and you still do your job. Make other arrangements this one time and let it go. But if the problem becomes chronic, your sitter is either sickly, doesn't want the job, or has histrionic personality disorder. Either way, you probably don't want her around your kids. Find someone whose problems are better concealed and/or only fucks up her own children.

10. **She invited her boyfriend over.**
    Is the boyfriend someone you know personally? Is he related to you by blood and/or marriage? Has he submitted to a criminal background check of his own and come through with flying colors? If your answer to ANY of these questions is no, then your sitter isn't dumb; she's insane. The only reason you let her text him all day long while she's supposed to be playing with your kids is so that he *never fucking comes over*. Shitcan her, yesterday.

Reminder! If kids are like iPhones, sitters are like chargers. Keep several backups around at all times, in case your primary one craps out, gets lost, or gets chewed up by the cat.

✻ **CHAPTER 19** ✻

This Is Why You Don't Homeschool: The Summer Reading List and Other Hallucinations

Last year, as the kids finished their final round of standardized testing, you decided you were fed up. *No child left behind? How about every child left behind?* You patted yourself on the back for that hilarious quip, then sprang into action. You set up a coffee date with Evangelical Mom down the block who pulled her kids out of public school after they did a kindergarten unit on bonobos. You also had lunch with Mensa Mom, who stopped enrolling her kids because the regular second-grade curriculum didn't include classical Greek, and really, how can concepts like democracy be fully understood without reference to their ancient origins? You didn't know what the fuck this meant, so you slipped in that your kids like pita bread and hoped that was kind of related.

But everything else she said totally resonated with you. *Teach your kids how to love knowledge. The world is your classroom.* So inspiring. Within a few weeks, you had some homeschooling resources and ordered a few grade-level workbooks for the kids. *That's it,* you said to Rufus, the family corn snake. *The kids are going to start learning for learning's sake!*

Rufus didn't hear you, of course, because corn snakes don't have ears. And that was your second mistake. Your first was assuming that the World Classroom would ever hire *you* as a teacher. You do have some experience with kids. Mostly the ones who came out of your own hooha. Your community college certificate in basic food safety is probably adequate to the task. But before you sign on, you might want to talk it over with Rufus again. Because if your summer parenting program is any indication of how good you'll be at teaching, you absolutely *cannot* do this job.

WHAT HAPPENED TO THOSE WORKBOOKS, ANYWAY?

You may recall that sometime in May, when you were trying to keep the family ship from falling into the hands of pirates, the homeschoolers sent you a big brown box. It sat on your dining room table until the first day of summer, when your kid—hoping it might be a new Wiimote—ripped it open. She learned five new vocabulary words, then started a unit on backyard entomology. In your homeschooling furor, you sent her out with a magnifying glass to inspect an anthill. She got too close and ended up with painful ant bites all over her arms. You felt so guilty, you bought her the new Wiimote.

* Answer: Workbooks still on the dining room table. One page completed.

WHY ARE KIDS SO DIFFERENT?

No matter what you eat when you're pregnant—or how many athletic skills you teach to the dumber one—you can't level the genetic playing field. They can have the *same* dad and still have different DNA. One of them may prefer to read dystopian fiction books in her free time, while the other one wants to bake. One of them may love to kayak, while the other one enjoys playing cards. One of them may be focused and nerdy and organized, like your spouse, and the other one has a high likelihood of getting a little too slutty when she drinks—you're not sure where she gets it. But the end result of this chromosomal crapshoot is that every time you suggest an educational family activity—art museum, folklore village, science presentation, free pottery demo—one of your unique individuals bitches about it until you give up. Time to crack open the workbooks.

* Answer: The only activity both kids like is watching the Disney Channel. So when they weren't doing worksheets, they mostly just did that.

WHAT HAPPENED TO ALL THOSE GRANDIOSE PLANS?

There are so many fun outings to do in the summer that it can be easy to confuse yourself with someone who will actually do one of them. Strawberry picking and family campout at the CSA farm, pontoon boating with your friends to the music festival on the lake, a minor league baseball game for kids' day, the butterfly exhibit at the botanic gardens. In real life, though, you can barely plan your afternoon in the morning. So of course, the one day you finally did buy tickets to the baseball game before it sold out, you told your son he could bring Rufus along and then forgot him in the car. In two innings, Rufus died of dehydration. At which point, you couldn't get your money back, and just went home.

* Answer: *Grandiose* means "excessively ambitious." A good vocabulary saves money. And lives.

HOW MANY BOOKS ON THAT "100 BEST NOVELS" LIST DID THEY READ?

When your friend, a children's librarian, sent you that link, you couldn't open it on your phone. Some format thing. Then when you remembered to check it on your laptop, you couldn't find it because your inbox was so cluttered with spam from companies whose spam list you intentionally joined to save 10 percent on your next purchase. When you finally found it and clicked on it again, your kid wasn't around to tell you which books she'd already read. So you ordered *Bridge to Terabithia* and *Blubber* and another one, then lost the original email when your fat thumb accidentally hit the Delete key. Why are these smartphones made for little troll hands?

* Answer: Definitely maybe three.

DO EDUCATIONAL APPS COUNT AS STUDYING?

* Answer: Obviously.

DID YOU GIVE THE KIDS AN INCONSISTENT MESSAGE THIS SUMMER ABOUT WORK?

Your husband thought the kid should get a math tutor. You think having a math tutor in second grade sounds about as fake as classical Greek. Whatever that is. Especially because—when you're not reading a clickbait article in the *Atlantic* about how hard it is to get kids into college—you think summer vacation should actually be vacation. Also, consistency requires effort. Sometimes you want to talk to your kids about geography, but most of the time you just want to sit on your ass and watch videos of Taylor Swift's cats on Instagram. Oh, Meredith. Such a grump!

* Answer: You better attend that August school enrollment. Because you're fired.

Reminder! Research suggests that every hour your kids spend in public school, they learn for only seven minutes. So homeschool them for fifty-six minutes a day, then wrap it up. Hey, it's 11 a.m. somewhere!

✻ CHAPTER 20 ✻

Your Only Goal Is Getting There: The Crazy Family Road Trip

Did you just agree to take the children to the state fair this weekend by yourself—while your hubby goes whitewater rafting?? Have you forgotten what happened the last time you put everyone in the car and drove halfway across the country? Whatever it was, it felt a lot like matricide. And you only survived it by feeding them the Disney Channel and locking yourself in the hotel bathroom with some lavender potpourri and a fistful of shit from the minibar.

What possessed you to agree this time? Perhaps it was the prospect of taking free rides on farm equipment. Perhaps it was the opportunity to sample fried cheese on a stick. Or perhaps it's because summer camps are finally winding down, and if you don't pack all these lunatics into the crazymobile and drive ten hours upstate, they'll surely end up as underage clients of the welfare state. Leave now, while they're still pre-orphans, but don't leave without a plan.

MANDATORY CONFESSION OF NOXIOUS FUMES.

There are some rules that children under the age of ten can't follow. You can try, for example, to ban the question "how much longer," but you will fail before you even get on the interstate, because kids are the hungry mountain lions of patience. Also, don't bother asking them nicely to use the bathroom when you stop. Tell them, not nicely. Because if they don't use it, they'll be asking you to stop twenty minutes later, when you're rounding the corner into Mirkwood.

But there is one rule you must enforce, and that relates to the *f*-word. Ten hours in the car with gassy children is intolerable. Most of us would rather take a road trip with people who don't believe in vaccines, and just came back from the polio region of Pakistan. Your kids need to keep you informed. **If** the perpetrator doesn't immediately confess to having "dealt it"—so the appropriate window can be rolled down—siblings are allowed to tattle.

EVERYBODY WEARS HEADPHONES.

Little kids have a tendency, when wearing headphones, to turn up the volume too high. While this tendency can lead to eardrum damage, there's only one person driving this car. And a lot more than an eardrum will be damaged if she veers off the road because motherfucking Farkle is screaming in the backseat. Speaking of screaming, no talking to each other when wearing headphones. Also, when kids stare too long at screens, they can no longer self-regulate their usage. So don't let them stop watching, or you'll have to deal with that.

BRING DRY SNACKS ONLY.

This may seem like an extreme position for someone on a fried-cheese pilgrimage to take. Especially since, just a few years ago, you banned dry snacks in the car on the grounds that the kids might choke. But even though they're older—and need to eat more—they're still just as messy and sloppy as they were a few years ago. Rules have to adapt with changing times. Better to face the small risk that they'll choke than the absolute certainty that you will have to wipe smashed banana and soggy coffee cake out of the cup holder at the end of the trip. Feeling dehydrated, kids? Have some more water. You'll be getting out to pee at the next stop.

PRACTICE GAMES OF SKILL.

Why is it that kids always want help with their skills at home, when you're busy reading *People* magazine? Help me tie my shoes. Help me braid my hair. Help me draw a three-dimensional box. Guess what, Napoleon Dynamite? You have ten hours to perfect those skills if you start right now.

Counting is a really great car skill to work on. Churches, cows, state license plates, green signs—it really doesn't matter what they count. Just set a really high random number—1,816 or higher—and tell them to get back to you only after they've reached it.

Once your kids have completed that challenge, ask them to make up a secret language. Kids love speaking in pretend dialogue. They're like improvisational comedians who aren't funny, and whose mouths make only one sound over and over. For this secret-language game, challenge them to make *no sounds*. In fact, see if they can play twenty questions using only sign language. Shhhh, Mommy's driving.

The one skill your kids **may not** practice is that of telling riddles or jokes. It's bad enough that you have to listen to the same jokes at the dinner table whenever a new relative comes to visit. But hearing them again, after five straight hours of unregulated eardrum damage—no way.

Reminder! A great single-parent driver game is called I Spy Nothing. In this game, all the people in the car except the driver close their eyes so they can't see anything, then try to spy things in their imagination. Bonus points for anyone who falls asleep during the game.

Managing Mommy Road Rage

If you take the kids on a trip, assume you will lose your shit at least once. But since your only actual goal on a road trip is getting everyone out of that car alive, you can't be raging on the interstate. Here's a list of safe people to scream at when you feel it coming on.

1. Starbucks barista. Or as you call her, the Starbucks fascista. You're at a rest stop on the highway. Does she really need to see your license with your credit card? When did Missouri turn into East Germany circa 1972? Take her down. No—first take your coffee, then take her down.

2. Truckers with girly wheel flaps. The only problem with yelling at these guys is they might be packing heat. Find one who's headed into the restroom and tell him (while he walks in) what you think of his denigrating wheel flaps. There's no reason to objectify the female body like that! Also, can't just one of these smutty companies make a wheel flap of Mark Wahlberg? Fucking patriarchy!

3. Husband. Why the hell did you agree to his solo man-rafting trip anyway? You know why. Because he scheduled it in the spring when you were still getting regular manicures. Now your fingernails look like toes and you're trapped in a minivan with skill-impaired people who don't know they're farting. Put the phone on speaker and when he answers, let him have it.

4. Audiobook Narrator. If nobody else is available, vent your frustration at the person reading your book on tape. Are you listening to a murder mystery, and the narrator's voice sounds like a cross between Idina Menzel and Beaker from the Muppets? Let it go, bitch. You can't hold it back anymore. When other drivers see you wearing headphones and screaming at your dashboard, they will swerve out of your way. Good. That perfect mom is gone.

✻ CHAPTER 21 ✻

The Last Week of Summer: The Final Frontier

If you've ever watched *Star Trek*, you know that the *Starship Enterprise* gets stuck in a lot of space anomalies. (If you haven't ever watched *Star Trek*, skip ahead to chapter 74: "Moms Who Have Never Worked a Night Shift, Never Smoked Pot, and/or Are Women.") What is a space anomaly? In the show, they're supposed to be atypical areas of space where highly unusual things happen. To most people, that sounds like a pretty good description of *all of space*. But that's what makes the space anomaly a perfect plot device. It explains nothing—and everything—at the same time. The ship lost power? Space anomaly. The crew has lost the ability to dream? Space anomaly. The time-space continuum is messed up and the captain just met his future self? Go ahead and take another hit off that bong. Also, space anomaly.

But dig this, Uhura. If you have an inexplicable sense of impending doom, and—no matter how hard you try to calm them down—everyone in your family is going bonkers, then you probably aren't watching a TV show about a space anomaly. It's probably just the last week of summer vacation. *This* anomaly is real, and it's a *total* clusterfuck. Here are some signs your family may be stuck in one:

* You feel like summer just started one minute ago.
* You haven't accomplished anything for ten weeks/one minute.
* You're happy school is starting because the kids need a regular schedule.

* You're sad school is starting because the kids grow up too fast.
* You feel like you should miss them more than you actually will.
* Your feelings are irrelevant because, kids.
* Your kids are excited for school because they're sick of summer vacation.
* Your kids are sad about school, because they love summer vacation.
* Your kids feel like they should miss you more than they actually will.
* Your husband, as usual, is completely unaffected.

A single encounter with your children may demonstrate any or all of these signs. Like when your daughter runs into your bathroom, without knocking, because she can't find her new bus pass. She brought it to her friend's house and left it there. You tell her she should've left it in her wallet, that you need her to be more responsible, and, by the way, you were GOING TO THE BATHROOM. She laughs at the phrase "mommy's privacy," then bursts into tears. You feel overwhelmed with guilt, go to hug her, and drop your smartphone in the toilet, so now you can't even call the friend's mom about the bus pass. Your husband is shaving in the other bathroom, completely unaffected.

If you see no obvious path out of this anomaly, that's because there isn't one. You're trapped until school starts, at which point you will transport yourself to the nearest juice bar and attempt to rebuild your warp core with wheatgrass and cayenne pepper. In the meantime, you may find yourself inadvertently personifying one or more of the following extraterrestrial life forms.

KLINGON

Your to-do list is killing you. After waiting in line for three hours at school registration behind a swarm of eighth graders with body odor, you sped to your other kid's "graduation" ceremony from animal camp, so you could watch her receive a shoddy certificate with the wrong name. By the end of the day, you feel like a crippled and captive warrior. In keeping with the spiritual code of your people, the Klingons, you could just perform ritual suicide and call it a day. But then who would take the kids to the drugstore for their combination locks? You must regain your combat strength. After the drugstore, swing by the new school and drop off the locks. Then go home and make dinner, freeze more food for next week, and throw everyone back in the car so you can look for the bus pass. If the friend's mom says she doesn't have it, assume she is a traitor and challenge her to a round of hand-to-hand combat. If you win, take *her* child's bus pass. If it's still light outside after the battle, go for a bike ride with the kids to get some ice cream.

VULCAN

Your kid's emotional hysteria is out of control. You tried to yell over him, but that strategy backfired. He's just yelling louder, and even with the door closed, you can't hear the online continuing education lecture that you are *totally* paying attention to. In these dramatic moments, you may find yourself instinctively calling on your Vulcan traits. Not the bushy, unkempt eyebrows. You'll take care of those when school starts. The Vulcan trait you really need is the one where you rely on reason and logic to solve problems. The kid is yelling, of course, because he doesn't want to take a bath. Logically speaking, hasn't this child had a bath *at least* every third day since he landed on this planet? It is true, he *did* just visit a farm full of sick and orphaned animals. Yet only a few diseases actually cross the animal-human barrier. He's probably at greater risk touching the faucet in his own bathroom, which hasn't been cleaned in weeks. You'll take care of that when school starts too. And right now, you really need to watch this TED Talk on health insurance so everyone can live long and prosper. Dump the bath.

BORG

If parents could solve every problem with logic, we wouldn't need to hide kale in blueberry smoothies. Let's say you just told your kid for the tenth time to clean up the dirty dishes that he hid under his bed, and he replied that he's reading a comic book and isn't "ready to clean up yet." Let's say he even *yelled* that. In your *face*. No problem! Because like everyone knows, yelling doesn't affect the Borg. In fact—because they primarily exchange ideas through collective audio messages—Borgs can't even hear yelling. They aren't big on biological distinctiveness or individual personality either. They have a hive mind. All they need is to communicate a few critical catchphrases, like *Resistance is futile*, and *You will assimilate or be eliminated.* If the kid is too comic book literate to eat his cereal in the kitchen—or clean up his rat-infested pigpen—it's time to go Borg on his ass. Failure to assimilate will result in his favorite snacks being eliminated. Period.

BETAZOID

You might be short-tempered, impatient, frustrated, and ready to kick your kids out of the Federation. But because you're a mom, you're also part Betazoid. Telepathically, you understand why they're acting like tribbles. Going back to school is a big transition. Their teacher might be nice. Or she might scream at them for going ahead in the textbook, and then rip up their extra credit in front of everyone and throw it in the garbage can. Teachers sometimes need Prozac too, and it's not easy to fire them. You'll have moments this week when your kids appear to be friendly aliens who are messing with your sanity because they're stuck in the anomaly with you. They want you to rescue them, but they don't know how to ask for help. Not politely, anyway. Use your "extra time" this week to talk, like a Betazoid, about feelings. Ask the aliens what is making them nervous. Ask them how you can help. If they are typical kids, they'll take this opportunity to disclose a bunch of feelings from *last year* that they never mentioned.

ARTIFICIALLY INTELLIGENT LIFE-FORM

It would be great if we could always be as calm and patient as androids and never lose our cool about long lines, dirty dishes, tubby time, or lost bus passes. It's actually kind of amazing that we don't lose it more often. Kids aren't easy. They have unbearably stinky feet, but we still take them shoe shopping. They leave a plush carpet of crumbs behind at every meal, but we still let them eat. They don't appreciate almost anything we do, but we still love them, beyond measure. And the real problem is, you can't program a robot to do what we do. Androids can't grow tiny humans with giant heads in their uteruses. They can't look at a kid's face and just know they're about to cry. They don't cheer at soccer games just because their kid touched the ball with her foot. One time. All season. As shitty as we are, Human Moms, we've still got a lot going for us. The last week of summer vacation is a complete clusterfuck, just like the rest of the year. Good luck. We believe in your mission!

Reminder! On *Star Trek*, lots of characters have mixed-race backgrounds. Like, Half-Klingon. Half-Vulcan. Half-Betazoid. Space moms uniting the Federation. You go, girls.

SECTION THREE

FALL

✻ CHAPTER 22 ✻

Your Babysitter Is Back in Session! Get the Kids Back to School so You Can Get Back to Life

Remember when you were a kid and you got excited about going back to school? Of course you don't. You haven't gone to school since mobile phones became a thing. Between cellular radiation and parenthood, most of your brain cells are fried. And the fact of the matter is, kids don't really get excited about going back to school. They get excited about getting *ready* to go back to school. So yeah, they're crunked up for *shopping*.

How can you snatch your life back from the jaws of summer vacation? The short answer is to manage their addiction. Or rather, *mismanage* it. Don't instill a love for learning or prepare them for the rigors of homework. You need to whoop them up into a back-to-school buying frenzy so extreme that by the time the first school bell rings, they are literally sprinting to the safe scissors bin. This is a little bit sneaky, and a lot like pimping. But it's only when they're back on the inside, compliantly reading books and being reminded ten times a day to use their indoor voices, that they will realize they've been duped.

BLACKMAIL THEM WITH SCHOOL SUPPLIES.

You haven't completed a full day of work—or had a single day at home alone—for months. Your lap dog misses you and, frankly, so does the couch. As fun as it was in the beginning, when the hot weather drove the kids outside to play hopscotch in the driveway, those days are gone now. It took them less than a week to figure out that the only game dumber than tic-tac-toe is hopscotch. Then they went to camp for a few days. Then they started bickering.

By summer's end, your offspring roam the house like a pack of wild hyenas, pouncing on each other at every sideways glance. No argument is too trivial.

It's my turn to hold the TV remote!

I set the table yesterday!

She's closer to the bowl of Ritz crackers!

As a tool for blackmail, school supplies never fail. That's because they are the skinny jeans of back-to-school shopping. No matter how bad skinny jeans look on you, or how uncomfortable they are to wear, you want them. They're so fucking *skinny*. You see them stacked up on the tables or rolled up in a bin like skinny denim tacos, and you instantly forget that they make you look—and feel—like ten pounds of potatoes in a five-pound bag.

That is exactly how your kids feel about buying new notebooks. The fact that you don't have legs like a baby giraffe—and your kid doesn't like copying down math problems—is irrelevant to the fantasy. And when it comes to buying stuff, kids are literally the world's biggest suckers. As soon as they focus their eyeballs on the twenty-five different varieties of writing implements, they are mentally transported into a Nickelodeon show in which they are straight-A students with cute hair and fresh kicks, blowing their classmates' minds with their multicolored ballpoint pens.

Need your kids to stop fighting? Prance into your home office and offer them a handful of chewed-up stick pens, dirty erasers, and stubby old pencils. Insta–peace treaty.

OR THREATEN TO CHOOSE THEM YOURSELF.

Depending on their age, your kids may realize your threats are hollow. You don't want to send them to school with short pencils any more than you want them to have stained clothes. Armed with a lifetime of inside information about your vanity, your kids ignore you. They race out to the car, start bickering about where to sit, and bang on the windows like angry inmates ready for their yard time.

Don't let these prisoners intimidate you. Remember that you have inside information too. Which is that their back-to-school fantasy works only when they can ponder, test, and systematically exclude every plastic three-ring binder in the store. You are not competent to make these selections for them because you don't know about their current favorite color, their aversion to paper binder dividers, or what their cool friends already bought. The mere thought of you coming home with forest green pens and sale-bin Hello Kitty binders will silence the rebellion. Be strong.

GET OLDER KIDS EXCITED ABOUT NEW CLOTHES.

Kids grow fast, huh? In your nostalgic moments, this makes you sad. From a logistical standpoint, it's just annoying, expensive, and unfair. By the end of summer break, you can no longer ignore the fact that their long pants are capris and—in some very dire cases—really should be cutoff shorts.

If your kids are boys, you can knock out this crap on your lunch break. If they're young, they want superhero underwear. If they're older, they want sporty shirts with logos like CAN'T STOP ME and WAY TOO FLY. Grab a few pairs of jeans and get back for your afternoon meeting. Girls, on the other hand, need a dedicated evening to roam around a store that plays bad pop music at an illegally high decibel and has a wide selection of faux-chinchilla sweaters decorated with peace signs, rainbow sequins, and random patches of eyelet lace. If your girl kid is a tomboy/lesbian, you can maybe just grab a few primary color shirts with peace signs. But if not—don't forget the awesome matching feather pens!

GET YOUNGER KIDS EXCITED ABOUT HAND-ME-DOWNS.

For younger siblings, back-to-school means a visit to that special store known as the broke-ass dresser in the linen closet. It's stuffed full of ready-to-wear examples of today's gender-bending fashion culture. What if your first-grade girl doesn't love navy blue Thomas the Tank Engine socks? Tell her that you understand her feelings. But she really has no choice, because you used up her clothing budget on that second round of fertility treatments.

There are ways to make this easier. Like, don't call the clothes "old" or refer to them as "hand-me-downs." Channel your inner used car salesman. Call these garments "certified, pre-owned" clothing. Tout their many superior qualities, as compared with the older sib's brand new stuff: *These shirts are already soft! These pants are label-free! They don't even have washing instructions, which is perfection, because they are also pre-stained!*

If your baby girl doesn't buy the hard sell, add some bribery. Offer her extra incentives and discounts. Like sole control of the TV remote. Her own bowl of Ritz crackers. The best seat in the minivan. If you're feeling WAY TOO FLY, throw in some vintage Superman underwear.

DON'T GET SO EXCITED THAT YOU MAKE SHOPPING BLUNDERS.

Don't worry that your kids will become materialistic. Too late. They already foam at the mouth over a Trapper Keeper. The bigger risk is that *you* will get caught up in your own fake frenzy and make some bad purchases.

* **An electric pencil sharpener.** Your kid will beg you for the sharpener. But keep in mind, he can't be trusted with this secret. If you buy a machine that speed-sharpens pencils, he will brag about it to the teacher, who hasn't had money in the budget for an electric sharpener since

the Bay of Pigs. She will lock onto your son's intel like a Chinese hacker, and you will spend the month of September sharpening every motherfucking seventy-two pack of Ticonderogas that walks through the second-grade door. Get the manual kind. Better them than you.

* **Refillable anything.** Were you high on rum cake when you went shopping? No, seriously. You got a ginormous package of lead refills for the mechanical pencils that your kid said she needed in four different neon colors. The other kid talked you into replacement shoelaces. Then you grabbed a few extra freezable inserts for the lunch cooler bags. Hope you saved your receipts. Because in a week or two—when the pencils are broken, the sneakers are stolen, and the lunch bag is lost—you will have a basement shelf full of untouched garbage.

* **"Rolling" backpacks.** Aren't backpacks so heavy these days? The poor kids are like hunchbacks. But remember that the same man who invented the rolling backpack probably also invented cobblestone sidewalks. And that man is a rotten dummy. The first time your kid leaps off the school bus onto an uneven stone sidewalk, those cheap plastic wheels are going to break off the backpack and go flying into your neighbor's fucking gladiolus. And you'll be stuck carrying the backpack—which is heavier than a normal one, because it "rolls"—all the way home.

Reminder! If your kid is the nerdy kind who actually loves learning, good for you. You've raised her right. But she still needs the cool pens. Nerds are materialistic now too.

✻ CHAPTER 23 ✻

The Neighborhood Carpool: Moms Do the Math

If you've ever wondered what people meant when they said that "the road to hell is paved with good intentions," look no further than the neighborhood carpool. The intentions are definitely good: Share the driving time, save gas. Yet inevitably—somewhere between the frantic group texting and the DQ Blizzard that the ADHD kid dumped all over your iPhone—you got rerouted to hell. You didn't buy that fucking minivan because you wanted to be a full-time chauffeur. You got it because your husband wanted a comfortable place to nap in the garage. And now you have way more seats than your own family needs.

In math, a good equation is one that's balanced on both sides of the equal sign. An equation that consists of one driver and seven passengers—none of whom would be useful in a medical emergency—is not a good equation. And it doesn't help that they're strapped down with seat belts. Physical confinement just makes their motor mouths more active.

Given this mathematical imbalance, the best way to think about carpool trips is to imagine them as *word problems*. You may not solve all of them. But at least your brain will stay more active than your saggy, inert carpool body.

GETTING EVERYONE THERE ON TIME

You need to get five kids to swim practice. You pick up four of them with ten minutes to spare. When you get to the McLatersons', however, nobody comes out. Should you wait in the driveway and pretend to be a patient person? Or should you throw the minivan in reverse and peel out backward across the lawn? To answer this question, remember that late people are always late. Seize the moral high ground. Send a passive-aggressive text to everyone on the carpool list, querying about a possible scheduling mistake. There was no mistake, and you know it. But this way, you'll be absolved of responsibility, and the late people will be publicly shamed.

GETTING EVERYONE THERE ALIVE

Try this equation. You're driving three boys and four girls to school. There are enough seats, but some kids have to sit next to members of the opposite sex. (Ewwwww.) You can configure them one of two ways: Put three girls in the way back and let the precocious girl sit with the boys. Or send all the boys to the back and make one girl sit in the front seat. Your daughter is short. If you got into an accident, she might well be decapitated by the air bag. Scary stuff. But she's the only one in the car you are legally authorized to place in harm's way. Tell the crash-test dummy to get in quick, so you have time to stop for coffee on the way to work.

PICKING THE RIGHT MUSIC

You're driving seven Girl Scouts back from an overnight camping trip. You try to shut them up with shitty pop music, but there's a problem. Every song is about getting drunk, having sex, or doing both at the same time in a nightclub. You're not sure those themes are appropriate for third graders. What if someone repeats the phrase "dirty rhythm" to a troop leader? She might take away their politeness badge. Then again, this is the same woman who requires your kid to dress up in an ugly brown socialist uniform and peddle cookies in a small-town strip mall. Nicki Minaj is crude. But at least she's not running a labor cult.

SHUTTING DOWN BACKSEAT DRIVERS

You're driving to band practice in a blizzard. Of course you are;

it snows every goddamn Wednesday, when you have to drive. Worse yet, the talkative kid who loves candy is also complaining about your driving. *We're going to be late if you keep going this slow*, says Kid Cuckoo Clock. You briefly consider speeding up and getting into an accident, just to prove that his high glucose levels are clouding his judgment. Instead, you keep your mouth shut. You are the adult in the car. The children's safety is your primary concern. Once you get there, however, focus on your secondary concern. Which is giving a bag of candy to every kid in the carpool who kept their fucking mouth shut.

WASHING THE CAR

On Sundays, you pick up from hockey. On Tuesdays, you pick up at soccer. On Thursdays, you drive home from karate. Overscheduling your children so they're never bored/home means your car seats are constantly smeared with muddy cleats, sweaty shirts, or grubby feet. This is better than having kids who are underachievers/have time to daydream. But from a practical standpoint, when should you get the car washed? Answer: In **fifteen years**, bitches. Your upholstery is nasty. It looks like it was buried at the bottom of a river with a dead gangster in it. It smells like the inside of a Diaper Genie. The only upside to driving this shit can around for the next decade is that when the kids eat dinner in the car—which they always do, because carpooling has replaced civilization—you never have to clean up after them. These apes get exactly what they deserve. And so do you, Lucy.

Reminder! Drive carefully. Never text in the car. Also, try not to be distracted by the orangutans in the backseat. If you've ever been to the zoo, you know that it's normal for them to throw food, pick their noses, and eat their own feces.

* CHAPTER 24 *

Braving the Bus Stop: A Field Guide for Anxious Moms

What is it about the school bus stop that brings out the crazy? Before the kids went off to elementary school, they took preschool field trips. You let them go because even though buses don't have seat belts—and that seems like a tragic lawsuit waiting to happen—you thought it was more important to keep your job than to keep your kids home.

Why is the big-kid bus so different? Well, for one thing, there are no teachers on it. Or chaperones. Unless you count the middle school kids who sit in the way-back seats, putting on makeup, cussing about homework, and throwing fruit cocktail out the windows. You think your "baby" already cusses like a third-shift nurse? Wait until the teenagers teach her sex words from Urban Dictionary.

Take a good look around. These other anxious moms can teach you everything you need to know about embarrassing your kids while they wait for the bus.

THE SPY WHO LOVED ME

Some kids—because they know their moms are worried and they don't give a flying fuck—insist on walking to the bus stop alone. Moms are considerate people, but that doesn't mean they're spineless patsies. As soon as he leaves, Long-Distance-Hovering Mom takes the dog for a walk. She follows her kid like Maxwell Smart, trailing him at a distance until he safely reaches the bus stop. If the kid turns around, she leans over and pretends the dog just pooped. Ah, the old fake-pooping-dog trick. Try waving to her. As soon as the bus arrives, she'll go home and deny she was ever there.

THE CAMERA-PHONE RUSE

You have to love a mom who takes a ten-minute video of her kid standing at a bus stop. Is there even room in the cloud for all this precious footage? Doesn't matter. Camera-Phone Mom will never upload these videos, anyway. She just needed an excuse to stand by her kid at the bus stop and micromanage him for a few more minutes through the lens of her smartphone. *Everybody say hi . . . Don't forget your locker number! OK, here comes the bus . . . I hope you have your lunch. There goes the bus . . . HEY, REMEMBER: DON'T TALK TO ANYONE WHO CLAIMS TO HAVE PUPPIES. HE'S ALWAYS A MURDERER. HAVE FUN!*

THE HALF JOKER

Ever since her kid was in the third grade—and asked her dad to start walking her to school—Needy Mom has couched her separation anxiety in jokes. Now she's got a whole new stand-up routine for the bus stop crowd. *Maybe I'll just run alongside the bus to make sure it gets there.* Ha! Ha! *Maybe I'll just sit in the back of your homeroom for a few weeks!* Ho! Ho! *Are you sure you don't want to hold hands right now? Just kidding!* Her jokes are meant to externalize and diminish her anxiety. Said her therapist. It's obvious to everyone, however, that underneath her nervous laughter is a crazy person ready to chase a bus. *That mom is such a riot!* Said no one.

THE MATCHMAKING FIX

Being *alone* is not the same thing as being *lonely*. Matchmaker Mom doesn't see it this way, however. She's blinded by maternal love/emotional projection. When she sees her daughter standing quietly by herself, Matchmaker Mom strikes up a conversation with another child who appears to be around the same age. Now that they "know each other," Matchmaker Mom beckons her daughter over. The girls stand together for a few minutes, then get on the bus and never talk again. The only thing they ever had in common, besides their mutual discomfort over Matchmaker Mom, was the bus stop.

THE MEET-THE-BUS-DRIVER GAMBIT

The way some parents act, you'd think their kid's twenty-two-minute bus ride was an epic historical moment. Like the storming of Normandy. And that makes sense, because, really, anything could happen on that long journey to freedom/school. The bus driver might miss a stop. A kid might pull the cord too early. Meet-the-Driver Mom, not willing to take that risk, climbs onto the bus to interview the driver. *What's your name? How long have you driven this route? How fast do you drive in residential areas? Are you a cigarette user? Do you ever take smoke breaks around the children?* Once she's satisfied that this bus driver is safe, sober, and making life decisions she agrees with, she disembarks. At which point, the bus is late for the invasion.

THE GPS-TRACKER TRICK

It's become increasingly common, once kids start riding the bus, for parents to give their kid a cheap smartphone. This makes total sense. Unlike in the olden days, when kids knew how to walk into a school building and ask to make a call—or to just sit their asses down to wait for the next fucking bus—kids today need their own telephones. But GPS-Tracker Mom takes this magic to an even higher level. Why should a kid waste his energy *calling* from the bus stop, when she can *see* him missing it—in real time—and jump in the car to rescue him? It's the perfect security system for wacky helicopter moms. It's a single-family Amber Alert, where the alert never sounds, because Mom is always watching, and nobody is (or ever was) in danger.

Reminder! If the kids don't get off at the expected stop, follow the bus—for thirty to forty-five minutes in your car—until they appear. Defeats the whole purpose of them taking the bus. But it's Crazy Mom, old school.

* CHAPTER 25 *

It's the Fall Harvest: Get Ready to Pick a Crap-Load of Apples!

Every fall, schools send home flyers about local places to go apple picking. Nobody knows exactly when the school district got on the marketing payroll of local apple farmers. They claim to do it "for the kids." In any case, now your kid wants to go. With the entire family. And you don't have to work this Saturday, so, unfortunately, that includes you.

Apple picking with your kids is a bit like eating dinner at Chuck E. Cheese. The kids run around trying to plunder every video game/apple tree in sight, while the parents chase after them carrying all their shit, because there's no safe/clean place to put it down. Talking your little locavore out of this fruit-hunting scheme won't be easy. When it comes to people believing everything they read, kids might as well be North Koreans. Don't cancel your massage appointment . . . yet. You have some propaganda of your own to drop: "The Half-Assers' List of Sucky Things About Apple Picking."

BAD WEATHER

Kids don't really mind rain. That's because they don't care if they get wet, until they do, at which point it becomes your problem to fix. Instead, focus on the *heat*. Unlike the pneumonia-hatching pumpkin harvest, apples rear their fibrous heads when places where apples grow are still hot. And not just hot but, like, **climate change hot**. And kids—whose resting body temperatures are just slightly cooler than molten lava—hate nothing more than being hot. Remind them how overheated they were, just yesterday, on the walk to school. Then repeat the words *walk uphill* and *heavy bags of apples* over and over until they surrender.

INSECTS

Kids don't care that their freshly picked apples typically come coated in pesticides. Everything does nowadays. Plus, they can't taste the toxic dust under the thick, gooey caramel. The reason commercial apple growers use so many toxic sprays is that almost every insect on the planet eats apples. Or lays their larva in the apples. Yummmm. Because a lot of kids are bug fanatics, they will look forward to seeing caterpillars, moths, and apple maggots. But you know how many kids like being stung by a wasp? Exactly zero. And how will your little guy feel about drinking that delicious apple cider when he's surrounded by a swarm of German bees? Go ahead, ask him.

FAUX-NATURE LOVERS

Getting kids outside and into nature is a worthy cause. But "nature outings" that involve hundreds of families taking separate cars to a seasonal weekend destination so they can save a few pennies on a bag of fruit is only slightly better than flying to the grocery store in a private jet. If your kids are honest, they'll admit they mostly just want to take a twirl on that rope swing. Well, honesty is a two-way street. Tell your kids that they will spend at least half their time waiting in line behind an impatient mob of toddlers, all of whom will be overheated and none of whom will get off the swing when their turn is over. How about a nature trip to the local playground instead, with a butterfly net and a chilled vodka gimlet?

THE ONLY BATHROOM IS AN OUTHOUSE

Only the most easygoing child will tolerate an outhouse. And chances are, your kid is not one of them. Your kid is the one who got scared by a fire drill at daycare when she was two and still can't use toilets with an automatic flush. Your kid also inherited her grandfather's strong sense of smell and gags at your morning breath. Has she taken any time to imagine how awful it will be when she eats a bunch of fiber and has to shut herself in that burning-hot shit box to relieve herself? If she hasn't taken the time, draw this mental picture for her. The outhouse is all the way down by the chicken coop, and it's got an even longer line than the swing does. The latch probably won't get stuck. But why take chances?

RANDOM MEDICAL EMERGENCIES

Apple orchards are not the most dangerous places in the world for children. That distinction belongs, in a two-way tie, to overseas sweatshops and backyard trampolines. But apple orchards are dangerous *enough*. For one thing, most of the apples you find at an orchard are actually on the ground—rotting. Round and slippery, rotters have no purpose in life except to ruin your kid's soccer season by turning her ankle. Also, apples are a choking hazard. Your kid may think, now that she's no longer a baby, that her esophagus can handle a bite of apple. And that may be true. Then again, kids don't drop their food nearly as often as babies do. So technically, they have even more opportunities to choke. Sound alarmist? Exactly.

Reminder! The worst thing about apple picking is that following the violent plunder, you always have too many goddamn apples. If you need creative ways to use those ten bags—that don't require you to make a pie crust—turn them into cocktail mixers. Apple syrup goes great with tequila!

✻ CHAPTER 26 ✻

Making a Healthy School Lunch Every Day: Never Gonna Happen. Don't Even Bother.

The standard American diet used to be so much easier to follow. Roughly half meat and half dessert, it was perfectly tailored for people who planned to die of a heart attack by the age of forty. But now that everyone is either a health nut or a foodie, dietary standards have become ridiculously high. Big Gulps have "too much sugar." Powdered cheese is no longer a "real food." You can't take your kids to the pediatrician without the nurse asking if your kid eats quinoa. Just nod. Nobody knows what the fuck that is.

Ultimately, advice on healthy food is a lot like the healthy school lunch itself: It works only if someone actually digests it. And kids, naturally, don't give a shit about their health. Why would they? We're talking about people who, up until about two minutes ago, believed in the existence of a tiny fairy that bartered teeth. Most elementary schoolchildren don't have a functional grasp on the difference between a suburb and a continent. These people are supposed to eat spinach salad and feel happy about it? Spinach tastes like chewy grass. Most kids would rather just go ahead and have the heart attack.

Here is some school lunch advice for people with lower—*realistic*—standards.

THE BEST LUNCH IS THE ONE YOU DON'T HAVE TO MAKE. Hot lunch in America doesn't always look that appetizing. The country of France exacerbated this already tenuous situation by posting pictures of its lunches all over the Internet. Thanks, Jacques Chirac. Then again, has anyone asked an actual French kid if they *eat* their fancy lunches? For all we know, Parisian schoolyard rats spend their nights feasting on discarded beet salad and Camembert cheese. More to the point, a hot lunch is not about impressing *children*. It's about giving parents one less thing during the work week that they have to stuff into Tupperware. It's not your fault if it sucks. It's also not your fault if it gets wasted, makes your kid physically ill, or gets thrown at the head of someone who calls him a bad name. Don't like it? Call your senator.

FUSSY KIDS GET PEANUT BUTTER (UNLESS THEY HAVE A PEANUT ALLERGY).

Remember when you were a kid and your parents told you to "clean your plate for the starving kids in China"? That slogan hasn't worked nearly as well ever since China took over our economy. But if you're one of those moms who gives your kid a peanut butter sandwich every single day of the week—because peanut butter comes in big jars and keeps in the pantry—you're in luck. Ever since a couple of smart French guys invented those nutritious peanut butter–based snacks called Plumpy'Nut to fight hunger in Africa, the new guilt for Western kids is peanut butter. When it's not killing people, peanut butter is literally saving the world. If your kid complains about her cold lunch *again*, give her two choices: She can either appreciate the fact that peanut butter is saving millions of children on the world's second-largest continent. Or she can start eating quinoa.

DON'T SUBJECT THEM TO LEFTOVERS.

In the entire world, only one group of people will eat lukewarm food from a plastic container. These people are *dads*. The rest of humanity prefers to eat food at the temperature it was originally served. Does our high standard of food preparation mean that we are all a little bit French? *Peut-être*. Throwing cold minestrone soup into your child's lunchbox might seem like the right move in the morning, when you're too hungover to find the peanut butter. But later, you won't have those leftovers for dinner, because that cold soup will be pooled at the bottom of the lunchroom garbage can with the rubbery dumplings, congealed potato casseroles, and lumpy curried rice bowls.

FRUIT SNACKS ARE VALUABLE, BUT NOT AS FOOD.

Some people believe that gummy fruit snacks are basically candy. What will they ruin for us next, cigarettes? Generally speaking, it's probably best to give kids actual fruit. Craisins, for example, only *sound* like made-up bullshit. They're a real thing and can be stored in the pantry. What you may not realize, however, is that fruit gummies are highly valued on the lunchroom black market. So if your pantry *is* stocked with fruit gummies—because one time someone told you it was fresh cantaloupe and you believed him—you can still give them to your kids to trade for *real food*. A bag of fruit gummies can be exchanged for cheese and crackers, sandwiches, wraps—even sushi! Kids aren't supposed to trade food. Then again, they also aren't supposed to push each other or talk in the hallways. You know why a bag of gummies is worth so much at lunch? Because that shit is *candy*.

A GLUTEN-FREE LUNCH IS NOT AN OPTION.

You did your best to instill in your kid a passion for gas station beef. But one day, she informs you that she'd like to "cut back on gluten." Look, every mom has her own limits. One mom may encourage her children to experiment with dietary restrictions. Still other moms may insist—based on a decent amount of anecdotal evidence—that vegetarians are actually witches. But following a gluten-free diet is a lot more extreme than just buying wheat bread or cutting back on lard-based frozen desserts.

Gluten-free people shop at special bakeries. Their default meal at a regular restaurant is an undressed salad. Unless she's willing to make her own Goldfish crackers from soybean starch and potato flour, your kid *will* eat gluten. She can start following a trendy diet just to keep her belly slim when she's eighteen and goes off to college.

Reminder! Making cold lunch at night is a great way to save time in the morning. But the best way to save time at night is to "forget" to make it, shrug your shoulders, and give them two bucks for hot lunch.

* CHAPTER 27 *

Don't Ask, Don't Tell: Speaking in Code When You Meet the Teachers

Sometime in the first few months of school, parents get a chance to meet with their children's new teachers. These meetings are typically called "parent-teacher conferences"—unless you bring your kids, in which case they're called "a complete waste of time." The point of these meetings is to get information and, at the same time, to impress the teacher in case she plays favorites. So it's a good idea to change out of your yoga pants and into something that looks less like pajamas. Also keep this in mind: You DO want to talk about how important your child's education is to you, but don't be too specific; at some point, your kid will admit that he didn't do his homework because he was playing *Call of Duty* late into the night with your boyfriend, and the teacher will know you copied those words off the Internet. The best way to make a respectable impression it is to speak in code and *never* say what you really mean.

SAMPLE QUESTIONS

Can you tell me a little about what my child will study this year? This question is a coded way to figure out how smart or dumb your child is compared with the other kids. The teacher knows this, and she will answer in coded language as well. If your kid is in the remedial reading group, expect the teacher to say something like "He'll be working on fundamentals." If your kid was deemed advanced but not *gifted*, the teacher will say, "He's exactly where he needs to be," or spuriously claim that "the groups are still being formed." At a general level, she will appreciate your interest in the study plan. But the operative words there are "a little." This isn't a hair appointment. You're not going to sit here for two hours with your feet on a stool while someone brings you magazines. You've got exactly twenty minutes to get a high-level overview of the curriculum and the schedule of standardized tests. Then it's time to get the hell out, because the Chen family's slot starts at 6:40 p.m.

Can I help in the classroom? When you ask this question, what you're really telling the teacher is that you intend to spy on her. Teachers are overworked and underpaid, but they're not dumbasses. They like to be in charge. Even if what they're in charge of is a bunch of sneezing children whose parents think they should be in the gifted math group. If you're in the classroom "helping out," you might catch the teacher rolling her eyes at a stupid answer, forgetting to set the standardized test clock, or referring to George Washington, in a moment of disrespectful candor, as a "silly-looking old white dude." The teacher can't let this intelligence circulate. Offer your help, but remember that you will still earn brownie points by doing menial labor in the photocopy room. You might even pick up some zesty gossip about the new principal.

My child is supposed to have educational goals? That's how the actual question will sound, but with a WTF tone of voice. When you were a kid, you were lucky if the teacher even knew your name. If you went to Catholic school, your main goal was to keep your mouth shut and never wear denim. In today's educational universe, kids are expected to take an active role. When your kid writes down his goals, he will say something totally abstract and shallow, like "make friends" or "learn math." That's because while teachers are professionally trained to set educational goals, kids can't even get their dirty socks into the hamper most nights of the week. Don't drop the *f*-bomb when your kid asks you what a goal is. Eventually, the teacher will tell him what his goals are supposed to be, how much time he has to complete them, and how far he fell short.

Do you have a school calendar? You don't ask this because you are going to put it on your nonexistent kitchen-wall planner. What you really want is for someone to look you in the eye and tell you *how many full weeks of school there will be this year.* With all the goal setting that goes on at schools these days, it's funny the school district hasn't established its own goal of *having more fucking school.* Regular bosses (silly old taskmasters that they are) expect employees to show up to work, FIVE days a week. But not at school! In that futuristic wonderland, almost every five-day week is truncated by a professional development day, a teacher comp day, or several consecutive days of ten-minute parent-teacher conferences. Could we stop compensating teachers with days off and just go ahead and pay them more? Why can't the school hold conferences during the first two weeks of school, when the only schoolwork kids are doing is learning names and cleaning tables? Why can't parents just email the teachers with questions, like they do with Amazon Prime? Also, why doesn't take-your-daughter-to-work day take place in the summer? Dammit, feminists! But don't ask the teacher any of these questions directly. She's still your best alternative to homeschooling, which would promptly knock your work schedule down from four days to zero.

Reminder! Teachers are not afraid to describe kids as hardworking and intelligent. If your kid's teacher uses adjectives like *fun-loving* and *sweet*, he's failing second grade. Time to get a tutor.

* CHAPTER 28 *

Who Ruined Halloween? Pretty Much Motherf*%king Everyone!

Just a few decades ago, Halloween was the ideal holiday for kids. They'd bob for apples, make a witch's brew with dry ice, and dress up for candy. Most of these activities were unhealthy. But that's why kids loved them. And so did moms. Any fuckwit could dress their kid in a bad homemade costume. You duct-taped a kid into a shearling vest, made horns out of aluminum foil, and called him a Viking. Or you covered a box with aluminum foil, poked holes in it for your kid's head and arms, and called him a robot. The costumes were ugly, but the fun was real, and, best of all, it required almost no effort. *You're going outside dressed in duct tape to beg candy from strangers in the dark of night? Sure thing, Thor. See you at bedtime!*

Today, Halloween is like the gluten of holidays. It's the source of everyone's fake stomachache. Let's take a closer look at the haters who fucked this up for us.

1. **Religious zealots.**

   In states across the country, religious people have gotten Halloween banned from schools on the grounds that it's about devil worship. Even though Halloween can be traced back to the ancestral worship of Celtic pagans, who were almost certainly too drunk to worship the devil, these religious folks believe that wearing a rubber zombie mask is basically satanism. So if you thought you could buy a pair of red plastic devil horns for your kid's Halloween party, think again. Someone may try to exorcise her from school.

2. **Nonreligious zealots.**
The mark of a truly dumb controversy is when different people lobby against something for opposite reasons. Hundreds of years ago, church leaders turned the day after Halloween into a holy day. Now, secular people say that Halloween is too religious and in the name of cultural inclusion have renamed it "Harvest Day." And thank goodness for that, because carving pumpkins and bobbing for apples is *a lot* like going to church. Don't send your kid to school in a bee costume made out of pipe cleaners. The principal might suspend him for violating the rights of devil worshippers.

3. **Sugar foes.**
Candy haters get up in our faces for some good reasons. American kids suffer from obesity, diabetes, heart disease, and hyperactivity. Letting a kid fill a plastic pumpkin full of sugary treats isn't exactly a lesson in health maintenance. But what lesson are they teaching with those self-righteous candy *buy-back* programs, when they take candy from kids and send it to overseas troops? You can eat candy only if you join the military? Soldiers don't need to follow heart-fucking-healthy diets? Kids don't deserve treats during wartime? How about if parents teach their own kids to regulate their sugar intake by sticking one piece of candy in their lunch every other day? Nope. Now you're a douchebag who's making soldiers cry.

4. **Sexy-costume makers.**
It's jacked-up that more people today *buy* their Halloween costumes than vote. Hmmm. Maybe Satan is behind this after all. Even worse than the store-bought costumes, though, is how they look. Really, who put the pedophiles in charge of making Halloween outfits for children? Because

those guys are killin' it. Parents used to dress their toddlers in cuddly bodysuits and furry hats with ears. Nobody wants to look at a little girl in that shit anymore. Now, kids can choose a Red Hot Devil outfit with tight red shimmer pants and a midriff halter. The sexy devil costumes might offend the religious community. But the creepy pervert community is *psyched*.

5. **Angry man-boys.**
Years ago, parents could take their kids to the YMCA for a kid-friendly Halloween party. Volunteer chaperones would put cold linguine in a bowl and pretend it was human intestines. It was stupid fake, and you could smell the pasta. But kids still got scared and went home. Send your kid to a spook house today, and there's a good chance that the guy selling tickets will be dressed in green camouflage pants and an orange vest that reads BEAVER HUNTER. Inside the haunted house, a fully grown man—'roided, bearded, and pissed about foreign-made hybrid cars—will jump out with a buzzing chainsaw. Your kid will pee his pants, literally. And instead of enjoying a relaxing evening out with your friends, you'll have to stay home with him on Halloween—every year—until he goes away to college. Thanks, Rambo.

Reminder! For some good old-fashioned shitty parenting fun, let your kiddos carve the pumpkins this year—by themselves! Hard, slippery squashes with hollowed-out interiors and a razor-sharp paring knife. What could possibly go wrong?

✻ CHAPTER 29 ✻

Nothing Is Funny at 4:30 a.m.: Coping with the End of Daylight Saving Time

Without a doubt, the best states in which to raise children are Hawaii and most of Arizona. It doesn't matter if you hate surfers, think turquoise looks trashy on white people, or have had a crippling fear of tarantulas ever since watching that one episode of the *Brady Bunch*. Hawaii and Arizona still kick the asses of all the other states because they don't observe daylight saving time (DST).

Daylight saving time was invented to save energy, not—as everyone believes—for the sleepy farmers. Farmers are an easy scapegoat. They're simple, and everyone knows they get up too early. In fact, the farmer theory is just as misleading as the one about the bus stop. Daylight saving *starts* in late spring and *ends* in late fall. The welfare of schoolchildren in America, as usual, is irrelevant to everything.

The worst part is, DST doesn't even save energy. Turns out, most people run their air-conditioning and incandescent lightbulbs whenever the fuck they want. So, why do we keep doing it? Well, the simple farmers are used to it now. Also, the government obviously hates parents, because the only parents who don't suffer from it are the smart ones who live in Hawaii and most of Arizona. And ***those*** moms.

THOSE MOMS

You probably met one of them at a book club once. It was early November. The book was *Gone Girl*. The gals were snacking on low-fat salami and sharing their own marriage-escape fantasies, and the conversation drifted to the topic of sleep deprivation. Someone announced that her kids have always been "good sleepers." Your first thought was, should children really get credit for performing a task that's required for basic survival? But when she reported that her kids are also "good eaters" and "good poopers"—and "never have trouble adjusting to daylight saving time"—you decided she must actually have a personality disorder. You smiled and politely nodded. Secretly, you wanted to punch her in the neck.

NORMAL MOMS

Normal moms don't have kids who "adjust" to the end of daylight saving time. You have kids who, having gone to bed at the normal time, now pop out of bed at 4:30 a.m., ready to start the day. You try to find some gallows humor in the fact that it hurts every bone in your body to be woken up that early on a weekend morning by someone who is simultaneously energetic, strung out, and needy. But you can't muster it. Why? Because *nothing is funny about kids getting up at 4:30 in the fucking morning*. You have only two responsibilities at this time of day. One, to lie on the couch. And two, to keep your kid alive. Hand him a box of dry cereal and gift him an extra [number of hours until 8 a.m.] of screen time.

DAYLIGHT-SAVING-TIME WARRIOR MOMS

While normal women counter their erratic sleep with dry Cocoa Puffs and publicly funded shows about police dogs, DST warriors rise to the occasion. Their emotional response to the clusterfuck of daylight saving time is to stand up and scream, *You want some of **me**, biOTCH?!*

Incremental change. According to the "slow adjustment" school of thought, you can prep your kids by tweaking their bedtime in fifteen-minute increments for several days in advance of DST day. If you think this tactic might solve your problems, great. But don't bother, because it won't. Nobody with small kids can reliably schedule their lives in fifteen-minute units. Before you commit, ask yourself why you're doing this. If you like the idea of well-rested children but mostly want to minimize your own pain and suffering, then fuck it. Take the lazy road.

Incentivize. In recent years, carrot-and-stick-parenting has fallen out of favor. It's no longer considered "good parenting" to respond to everything your child does with either a reward or a consequence. The attachment parents did this to us. They did it with their baby slings and their empathy and their circle jerks of breastfeeding. And now it's time to fight back. Bankers have bonus structures, why the hell can't kids? Give your little Rockefeller a bonus for every minute he stays in bed past the "fall back" time. It doesn't have to be money. Kids will also leap through hoops for gum, candy, upgraded apps, or R-rated movies. Not only will incentives keep him in bed for between two and nineteen minutes longer every day, but also you'll be teaching him the palatable corporate value of making a profit by doing almost nothing. Win-win!

Disincentivize. Some kids are incapable of being carroted or sticked. Maybe they're in kindergarten and haven't done the time-telling unit. Maybe they're afraid of the dark. Maybe you tried attachment parenting for about a minute, realized that toddlers don't have the cognitive capacity to learn empathy, and reverted to bribing them for any small change in behavior, and now they just tune you the fuck out. Your kid won't stay in bed for a carrot, because she knows she'll get candy for doing something even easier later. She won't stay in bed for a stick, because she knows you'll give the screen time back later, when you need to give her a carrot. Stay a step ahead of these corporate drones with more creative disincentives.

1. **Climate change.** Explain to your child at bedtime that you take the *saving* part of DST very seriously. Anyone who gets up before the "new time" has to have an invisible carbon footprint. No screens. No hot water. No lights. Even opening the refrigerator for a glass of chocolate milk is forbidden—waste of cold air. If your child protests your draconian environmental stance, show him a picture of a polar bear stranded on an ice floe. Tell him you're doing it to save the bear, then start saving for his therapy.

2. **Blaming the farmers.** Tell your kid that, because of the sleepy farmers, everyone in the family—except the ones who stay in bed—has to go outside at 4:30 a.m. and pull weeds. If the weeds are already dead, give him a broom, send him into the garage, and make him pretend it's a barn. Nothing like an extra hour of cleaning time in the morning before you wake the cows.

3. **Philosophy lecture.** Deliver a lecture on the social construction of clocks. Start with the preindustrial age, when people worked according to task, instead of time. Talk about the invention of Greenwich Mean Time in 1847 and work your way forward into the digital age. Anyone who doesn't want to listen to your drivel has the option of staying in their bed and lying motionless in the dark.

Reminder! Spring: Forward. Fall: Back. Winter: Find out who invited the obnoxious woman with great sleepers to book club. Summer: Unfriend both of them.

⁂ CHAPTER 30 ⁂

Miserable Bitches Unite! The Annual PTO Fundraiser

School fundraisers. So fun. Sometimes it can be hard to know what you look forward to most. Is it that you get to wait behind a counter to serve food to impatient assholes for zero compensation, just like you do at home? Or, is it that you get to do all this thankless work on your only day off with some of the most miserable bitches in the world: your fellow moms? Hard to say.

Put a bunch of moms in a room together to cooperate on a project involving children—some of whom are their own, and the rest of whom they don't actually like—and they will eventually turn on one another. Stay-at-Home Mom will launch an unsolicited diatribe about the importance of family dinners and the "work-life imbalance." Single Mom will respond with a comment about primary caregiving that includes the words *boredom*, *privilege*, and (in air quotes) "*working*." Full-Time-Job Mom would agree . . . if she were there. But conflicts like these are just the low-hanging fruit. If you want to volunteer at your kid's school, gird your lady loins. Those PTO bitches don't play.

HIGH-POWERED FINANCE MOM

She's a tiger mom, Asian or otherwise, and she just got laid off. After working one hundred hours a week for fifteen years, she suddenly has a lot of free time. In a relaxation-induced *panic*, she signs up for every shift at the PTO hat sale. She shows up in pumps and a blazer, wielding a clipboard. When she finds herself surrounded by women who are wearing jeans and sneakers, she assumes they are nannies and starts giving them orders. After ignoring their polite efforts to make conversation, HPF Mom gets offended when one of the nannies asks her to hang up vinyl signs. She could obviously be running this whole operation! She performs one menial task, leaves the building, and never shows up for her twenty other shifts.

HIPPIE/COUNTERCULTURE/RASTA MOM

Hippie Mom has a relaxed attitude about everything. Requirements. Schedules. Haircuts for her sons. Because she's so mindful and accepting and calm, Hippie Mom is always happy to pitch in for the community. But don't be surprised when she shows up late, brings both her kids, and immediately asks for a chair. Not for herself, of course, but for the four-year-old she's carrying in her East African baby wrap. Good news is that he's almost weaned. Less helpful to your fundraising effort is that after reorganizing the seating for ten minutes, talking with her older kid about his anger for ten minutes, and then calling her Reiki therapist to set up an emergency session, she has to leave again. Living 100 percent in the present, she suddenly remembered the future is coming. It's her turn to host the drum circle and she hasn't even made hummus yet. Peace. Out.

HIGH-MAINTENANCE MOM

It's ten minutes until the doors open, and the tablecloths aren't on the bingo tables yet. The games director asks the mom who's doing nothing, to do that. But you soon understand exactly why she was doing nothing. There's nothing she can actually *do*. Or at least, nothing she can do without asking for your help. *How much of the table should I cover? Should the tablecloth be taped down? Do you want the colors to alternate? Are the bingo boards supposed to be underneath the tablecloth like this?* OMG, are you a congenital asshat? You don't say that to her, but you can't help thinking it. Because every time High-Maintenance Mom asks a question, you have to stop doing your own task and do hers. She's really sweet. You want to feel grateful for her assistance. But wouldn't it be more efficient for everyone in the PTO and the whole goddamn world if she just went home and fucked up her own tablecloth?

OCD MOM

At her day job, OCD Mom is an anesthesiologist. Being slightly obsessive-compulsive is a perfect quality for someone who is mixing codeine cocktails for surgical patients. Sometimes the school also benefits. Nobody else wanted to organize Tupperware in the teacher break room. So many mismatched lids! She brought her labeler to the art fair so that the pom-pom balls wouldn't get thrown in with the felt scraps. Major crafting chaos! She's *really* good at setting up tablecloths. Just don't give OCD Mom a task that needs to get done quickly. Like face painting, where there's always a long line, and there's no time to sanitize the brushes in between customers—or to start over if the paint smudges. It's a miniature cheek, Dr. Strangelove, not a critical chest wound. Wasn't that uptight bitch with the clipboard supposed to work this shift?

GOODY-TWO-SHOES MOM

Remember that girl in seventh grade who always warned you against making a bad choice? Truth is, she was usually right. That roof was *way* more slanted than it looked. Boys *don't* delete boob shots. Fast-forward thirty years, and GTS Mom still knows everything. She has no greater passion than her kids, and she spends all her available time volunteering at the school. She also thinks you're a brainless cretin, and keeping that information to herself would feel, to her, like being wrong. When you asked where the popcorn machine was stored, she rolled her eyes. When the upright piano toppled over onstage and you giggled because the music teacher started crying, she reminded you that the school can't afford another piano and questioned your shallow ethics: *A child could have been killed.* Never mind that no children were onstage. Break it up, everyone. Fun is over.

PERPETUAL-OUTRAGE MOM

She used to be a teacher of some kind. Now she uses all her available intellect to complain—in regular letters to the school administration—about the educational system. She's here to help. But mostly she's here to bitch. The fundraiser is the perfect opportunity, because she's surrounded by people who might also be angry—about the school's lack of transparency, its pathetic library, the absence of talented and gifted resources, and, of course, standardized testing. *Does the principal even follow the debate on testing?! Has he read the latest research on mainstreaming? Doesn't it seem a tiny bit suspicious that he funded the unicycle club and then cut the afterschool program in European languages?* That last comment makes you wonder whether her outrage is a little bit Aryan in flavor. But mostly, you want her to stop. You can't solve these problems right now. You have to solicit donations for the pathetic library.

BAD-HYGIENE MOM

It might be a cultural thing. Or a religious choice. You don't really care, and you don't really judge it. All you know is that the gymnasium is hot and stuffy, and you need to REMOVE Bad-Hygiene Mom from the premises. There's more air circulating in the hallway, near the front doors. Give her a job out there. How about hanging up posters? If she protests that she is only four feet eight, tell her you want the posters at shoulder height. Or send Goody-Two-Shoes Mom to assist her. Bitch *totally* had that coming.

FUNDRAISING-DIRECTOR MOM

While other PTO positions rotate from year to year, this woman does the same job year after year. She can't *stand* doing it, but with an even greater passion, she can't stand the idea of someone else fucking it up. One year, Fundraising-Director Mom comes up with an ingenious plan for a big harvest fair. The playground is filled to insanity, and the lines stretch out onto the sidewalk. Just then, some diva mom with an art degree shows up to complain that she can't *possibly* work the dunk tank unless she is provided with a shade umbrella. *Human skin is like an art canvas,* she says. *It must remain supple and taut.* FD Mom blows a gasket, slaps the diva across the face with her Stanford MBA, and resigns. The following year—when the school ends up with a ten-thousand-dollar shortfall—everyone finally understands how good she was. Well, at least nobody got sunburned.

Reminder! You know how you can bitch about your kids, but if someone else does it, you immediately classify her as backward or sexist? That's how Fundraising-Director Mom feels about people who mock her fundraiser.

✻ CHAPTER 31 ✻

The Thanksgiving Holiday: Who's Up for Chinese Takeout?

If only there was a holiday that allowed moms to plan a menu for two weeks, cook for four days, and clean the whole house, so that they can sit down for a total of eight minutes before getting up again to refill water glasses, fetch pie, or settle a conflict at the kids' table. OK... No... Come to think of it, that sounds like every holiday.

But isn't Thanksgiving the worst? Because on Thanksgiving, the sole focus of all the work is eating. That's literally the whole point. Nobody atones. Or exchanges presents. Thanksgiving is just a huge domestic chore *on steroids*, done for the sole purpose of letting everyone else feel thankful about stuffing their faces. Thanksgiving was obviously invented by men to celebrate a short workweek that ends in three of their favorite things: carbohydrates, football, and sitting.

Unless you have the kind of male spouse who enjoys picking out the wine, arranging the cornucopia centerpiece, and playing charades with his parents—in which case your spouse is *totally fabulous* and/or might be gay—it's not a "holiday" for you. You don't have to be Native American to appreciate the fact that Thanks*giving* actually involves a lot of *taking*. But then, what's a shitty American mom to do?

DECLARE A REFORMATION.

When Henry VIII was king of England, he wanted a divorce from his wife, Catherine of Aragon, so he could make Anne Boleyn his second queen. The Catholic Church (natch) wouldn't let him.

Henry responded by starting the English Reformation. Things didn't work out that well for Anne Boleyn. Old Annie crossed the rainbow bridge. Headless. But the point is this: It was supposedly during the English Reformation that people started observing "Days of Thanksgiving" to celebrate special events. Like the birth of royalty. And victory over Spain. The Reformation was invented to ratify divorce. Isn't it time we all returned to the culture of Mother England and just left our (first) families on Thanksgiving?

PARDON YOUR TURKEY.

If getting divorced seems like an unnecessarily drastic solution, you may wish to pay homage to a more recent, homespun cultural tradition. Every year, our president picks a turkey and pardons it, so it won't be executed for someone's dinner. Given all the debate about overcrowded prisons, maybe the president should just skip Thanksgiving and go ahead with pardoning an actual person. But we're not here to debate the meaning of democracy. We're here to complain about national holidays. Celebrate the chief executive way: Pardon a turkey. In fact, pardon the whole meal and get some Chinese takeout. What the hell? It works for Jewish people on Christmas.

CELEBRATE BLACK THURSDAY.

We are a country that loves its brined meats and comfort foods, but we are also a country of consumers. Every year, it seems, the stores open earlier and earlier. Perhaps we should all just give up and give the capitalists the whole weekend. Start your Black Thursday at the grocery store, serving your family a traditional Thanksgiving meal out of reinforced cardboard boxes. Following that consumer binge, go buy a new TV, a few video games, some diamond earrings, and a smartwatch. You may miss the ritual of sitting down together and giving thanks. But won't the fam be even more thankful to get a bunch of new shit for more than half the regular price?

RUN BACK-TO-BACK TURKEY TROTS.

All we hear about from doctors and political leaders is how we eat too much and don't get enough exercise. We would obviously be better off as a country if we celebrated Thanksgiving on a running track. Instead of signing up for one turkey trot, try four of them! The whole family will be so exhausted that by the time you get home for dinner, nobody will be able to lift a fork. Also, November weather is icy and cold. If one of your kids ends up with hypothermia—or Grandma fractures a hip on a patch of black ice—you could end up spending all day in the ER. Line it up, hospital food!

GO WITH THE NUCLEAR OPTION.

It's party time, pilgrims. Invite everyone you know and tell all of them—regardless of gender, religion, felony status, fitness level, or closeted sexual preference—to make a dish. With everyone pitching in, you might even get to focus on eating—turkey, honey ham, Cornish hens, corn on the cob, mashed potatoes, sweet potatoes, potato salad. Thirteen types of gravy and fourteen varieties of stuffing. Green beans. Collard greens. Green salad. Fifteen pies. Banana pudding. Red velvet cake. Wine. MORE WINE. With all those people in your house, you'll have to figure out where to serve the kids. Wait. Kids? Send them down to the basement to watch all the Harry Potter movies. You are thankful for your kids. But c'mon. Not when they're at the dinner table.

Reminder! The day before Thanksgiving is one of the busiest travel days of the year. Pack up to visit relatives, and you might just end up spending the night on an airport bench or floor. If you want to feel true gratitude this Thanksgiving, pack yourself a portable army cot.

* CHAPTER 32 *

Five Good Reasons Not to Chaperone Your Child's Field Trip

The first graders are going to the geology museum, and your kid really wants you to chaperone. You can't go, you tell her. You've got a big meeting that morning. *Do you really have a big meeting, Mom?* Don't buckle under these harsh interrogation techniques. You have good reasons for skipping that she can't possibly understand.

1. **You'll miss a catered lunch from your favorite restaurant.**
   OK, a catered work lunch is not technically a "big meeting." But you ordered your selections weeks ago. You normally satisfy every sad stereotype that French people have about Americans by having a cold sandwich with tap water at your desk. Skip the linguine with clams for glowing rocks? Fuck that!

2. **You want to miss snot, poop, rats.**
   It's an axiom of school field-tripping that something abnormally gross will happen. At the sculpture park, a kid wiped green phlegm on your shirtsleeve. At the children's museum, a toddler threw his poopy diaper into the wave pool. At the pumpkin patch, the first pumpkin you picked up was rotted and filled with rats. You don't need this shit. Not on catered-lunch day.

3. **Suck it up, kid. This isn't the Hunger Games.**
   Your daughter likes dolomites, because she's half nerd. But

she's also afraid of the dark, because she's half chicken shit. But really, Katniss. What's the worst that could happen to you in the Hall of Glowing Rocks? Even if things get a little messy in there for a minute, you'll probably come out alive. May the odds be ever in your favor.

4. **The other chaperone is Carol.**
   Every so often, you sign up to chaperone and get stuck with a mom who's even lazier than you are. But at very least, you need to be fully engaged in the task of not losing kids. If Carol runs out of the dinosaur exhibit to hop on a work call—and leaves you to watch her group of rambunctious boys—you can't be certain of your head counts. So much for lesbians and sisterhood.

5. **School buses are abnormally bouncy.**
   The geology museum is downtown. There's no parking on the street. And sorry, but school buses are germy, smell like cafeterias, and emit nasty exhaust fumes. They're uncomfortably bouncy and have a terrible turning radius. Also, school bus drivers are almost never friendly, which is also uncomfortable, because it makes you wonder what job they'd rather be doing and couldn't get. Let's reconvene after school.

Reminder! Even if these five reasons didn't apply, there would still be another: the geology museum gift shop. Every time you go, your kid howls for the fancy rocks, then promptly leaves them in the car. Your car is not a quarry. The answer is no.

✻ CHAPTER 33 ✻

Five Good Reasons to Chaperone Your Child's Field Trip

Your fifth grader asks if you plan to chaperone her trip to the climbing gym. *Please don't chaperone the field trip*, she says. *I just want to hang out with my friends... alone.* Don't absorb this negative energy. You have good reasons for going that she can't possibly understand.

1. **Good information is scarce.**
   By fifth grade, teachers don't need as much help in the classroom. When you ask the kid what happened at school, she just says, "Stuff." When she was smaller, you could run an errand during morning recess and slow down to five miles per hour near the school playground. But now you can't risk being seen. She knows what a helicopter parent is and believes you should trust her. You totally don't.

2. **Older kids can blow their own noses.**
   Chaperoning a class of proto-babies is real work. Even the ones who *try* to be good listeners have a 62 percent chance of stepping off the bus and falling right into a sewer. Bigger kids have more self-respect. You might have to untangle them from a climbing rope once in a while. But if anything unexpectedly disgusting happens, they're too embarrassed to ask for your help. Game on.

3. **Every field trip is a high-stakes negotiation.**
   Little kids are unreasonable. They ask you to chaperone

the pumpkin patch trip. Then, when the geology museum happens, they ask you again. It's like borrowing money from a loan shark who constantly raises his interest rates, then flings his body down on the floor like an angry starfish. Your tween understands how negotiation works. If you come this time, then you don't have to take the swim team to the waterpark. You can stay home, and she can wear a two-piece. Climbing gym, FTW.

4. **If you think it's bad now, just wait.**
   Parenting a tween sometimes feels like the calm before the storm. It's actually the windy day before the F5 tornado. You think your kid acts like Sybil now? Wait a few fucking years. By high school, she won't even bring the chaperone form home. She'll just sign up for the ski trip and return late Friday night high on glue. Take advantage of the time you have with your slightly obnoxious child. Pretty soon she'll be a full-blown narcissist with a private Instagram account.

5. **Pimp your ride.**
   As the kids get bigger, the bus gets more crowded. *Bummer.* You stop for coffee, check your Facebook in the parking lot, and leave your purse in the car. Later, you grab lunch with Carol, then take the rest of the day off. Why not? You chaperoned the shit out of that field trip, and you don't have to catch the bus. Cheers, Carol!

Reminder! Always sign up to chaperone a field trip on the last possible day. With any luck, the spots will be filled, and you'll still get teacher points for offering.

SECTION FOUR

WINTER

✻ CHAPTER 34 ✻

Cold and Flu Season: Tired Old Wives' Tales for Tired Old Wives

If you're still looking for an excuse not to chaperone, here's one more. No sooner will you turn in that check for $4.25 than your kid will be sent home with a fever. So even though you just took the day off to chaperone, you now have to tell your boss you're missing the quarterly review. Kudos to you, school nurse. *Your* job will still be there on Monday.

Cold and flu season starts in October. By early December the pathogens are spreading faster than holiday cheer. Ironically, holiday cheer helps spread the contagion. You better hope someone spiked the punch at your work party, because the punch ladle was also carrying influenza B.

From October to April, children are basically sick all the time. But you can't even yell at them for it because, unlike with broken bones—which kids foist on themselves by being simultaneously fragile and reckless—germs aren't really their fault. Between the parents who don't vaccinate, the parents who send their sick kids to school, and the teachers who don't provide hand sanitizer because they prefer diarrhea to contact dermatitis, every door handle is a repository of infectious disease. Until American schools require kids to wear hazmat suits and burkas—neither of which is currently available with superhero logos or sequins—kids will catch it all. Try to find some wisdom in these old wives' tales, revised and reinterpreted for modern use.

STARVE A FEVER, FEED A COLD.

This myth has been around since Christopher Columbus

discovered India. Back then, it was common medical practice to put a hot iron on hemorrhoids. Also, having a fever was basically the same thing as dying. A European serf child might catch a passing virus and get over it, but it was more likely he had the bubonic plague. Given the odds, why not just starve the kid? Now that kids can survive viral and bacterial fevers, the starving thing isn't really necessary. In place of *starve*, you can substitute *ignore*. Because if your kid is home with fatigue and muscle aches and a weak appetite, he is probably content to lie on the couch watching movies. *Starve him of your attention* and get some work done. Shit's gonna get much more medieval around here if you lose your job.

SNEEZE INTO ELBOWS, NOT HANDS.

This isn't exactly an old wives' tale. But it should be. It's good common sense. Sneeze into your hand? Who does that anymore? You might as well sneeze right into someone's mouth and then—just to be sure the hepatitis got in—hock a loogie into their eye. An important but lesser-known strategy is *wiping your nose into your elbow*. Maybe it's more sanitary to use a tissue. But WTF—your kid is already there to sneeze. There are already germs in that arm crevice. Plus, the sneeze dislodged the mucus, which was God's plan all along. Tell the kid to go for the trifecta and do everything on the same "Kleenex." For really bad colds, he might want to alternate arms, to give each sleeve the time it needs to crust over and dry.

KIDS ARE CONTAGIOUS BEFORE THEY HAVE SYMPTOMS.

Know those parents who get mad when their kid catches a virus from yours? Poor control freaks. They must have a terrible time playing Chutes and Ladders. So maybe you shouldn't have sent your daughter to their house with a stomachache. Little Madison was up all night barfing, and missed her own birthday party. And you'd feel worse about that, if your kid had been invited.

Really, though, this kind of viral defensiveness is only excusable in new parents, who have yet to figure out that kid germs are a game of Russian roulette. Your kid *might* have given that girl her virus. Or that girl might be sick with a different virus. But even if it is the same one, it's not a foregone conclusion that she got it from *your* kid. It might've been the spitty kid who sits next to her in music class. And for all you know, Madison might be sick with something that hasn't presented yet and just gave it to your kid. Everyone just chill the fuck out and put the gun to your head.

IT'S ALMOST ALWAYS A VIRUS.

One reason moms feel like they fuck up a lot is that every once in a while—when you actually do—your kids never let you forget it. Like the day it was ten degrees outside and your daughter said she was "too tired" for her ski lesson. You made her go because you'd already "paid for it," and she ended up having "strep throat." Well, nobody's perfect. But also: That almost NEVER HAPPENS. Most of the time, you let her skip the lesson and—because you're a pitiful love-struck sissy—you rush her to the clinic on the other side of town to get her tested for strep throat. And of course, the rapid test is negative. *It's viral*, the doctor says. She knows you're disappointed and will ask for antibiotics anyway. But if she's responsible, she'll say no. It's always viral, and it will be every time, right up until you nut up and make the kid do the lesson again, with pneumonia.

YOU CAN GET SICK IF YOU DON'T WEAR A COAT.

Every year, parents debate the relative merits of outerwear. Did he get sick because of a virus? Or did he get sick because he was outside without a coat, and he got a virus, and his immune system was compromised by the cold? Nobody really knows for sure. And everyone is different. So you might as well take the cover-your-ass approach and drop this on him: He got sick because he didn't listen to you. One way or another, it's probably true anyway.

WHINING IS THE SIGN OF AN EAR INFECTION.

Some parents say that they always know when their kid has an ear infection, because the kid "acts different." He cries for no reason, he whines nonstop in a high-pitched voice, he wakes up in the night, and he refuses to participate in normal activities. Other parents think those behaviors describe how their perfectly healthy children act every single day. If you are one of those parents whose child whines only when he has an ear infection, you should never complain to anyone about cold and flu season. You should never even complain. Also, everyone hates you and your child might be a hologram.

FOLLOW THE BRAT DIET.

This is such an easy target that it almost seems criminal to include it. **BRAT**—an acronym that stands for **B**ananas, **R**ice, **A**pplesauce, **T**oast—was invented to help parents remember what to feed kids when their tummies were upset. Rumor has it that BRAT was actually the second choice of doctors. Their first choice was **S**top **T**he **D**iarrhea, but pediatricians didn't love using the acronym **STD**. In the end, they should have just called it "chicken fingers," because about three minutes after everyone learned it, doctors threw it out. Give your little sicko binding foods, or anything he wants. BRATS, ALL. Easy to remember, isn't it?

Reminder! Vaccines don't cause autism, but ignorance does cause polio.

* **CHAPTER 35** *

The Solstice Sucks! A Winter Survival Quiz

You got through autumn without losing your job or ripping out anyone's weave in the school drop-off circle. Life is good. But now the winter solstice—the shortest day of the year—is fast approaching. Even if your kids can downhill ski by themselves while you sit in the ski lodge snorting s'mores, winter is not all fun and games. It's mostly just games. Lots and lots of board games, in the living room. Are you worried you might spend the next three months playing the game of Life instead of actually living it? Evaluate your winter readiness by taking this quiz.

1. **How to shop for winter boots**

   Your kid's feet grew nine inches in a year. You decide to…

   a) rush to a nearby store while there's still a good selection.

   b) squeeze his feet into the old ones for a bit longer.

   c) order boots online.

   d) give him your rain boots, with three pairs of wool socks.

   The correct answer is *a, b, c,* and then *d,* in that order. At the shoe store, your kid tried on seventeen pairs of boots. Two weeks later, someone walks off with his boots at an ice rink. He wears the old ones until the Internet boots arrive, but he refuses to wear them. Cue the wool socks.

2. **How to build a snowman**

   It's the first snowfall of the year. Your kids are excited and want help building a snowman. You say…

a) "Totally, that's a great idea!"
b) "Yes, I will. I'd love some fresh air."
c) "Well, I could use some exercise."
d) "You get started, and I'll join in at 4 p.m."

The best answer is *d* because at 4 p.m., there are only twelve more minutes of daylight. That's just enough time to find a corncob pipe and go back inside.

3. How to eat yellow snow

Your kid is playing with his friend in the front yard. When the friend dares your kid to eat some yellow snow, you...
a) explain that dog urine is not safe to eat.
b) run out with red dye #40 and offer to turn it orange.
c) double-dare the friend to do it instead.
d) sit back comfortably, relieved it's not brown.

The answer is *anything except b.* Kids have been eating dog-pee slushies for decades. Synthetic food dyes, on the other hand, are carcinogenic. Organic Mom knows best.

4. How to do winter travel

Your spouse has to travel to Florida for work and suggests you bring the kids for a quick beach vacation. You say...
a) "Can't wait to soak up the sunshine!"
b) "I guess they can miss a few standardized tests."
c) "Bitch, did you just say 'vacation'?"
d) All of the above.

The answer is *d.* It's a biological fact that humans need sunshine, that there will be more standardized tests, and that taking kids to a beach by yourself is not a vacation. Spouse isn't taking a trip. Spouse is trippin'.

5. How to go sledding

You promised to take the kids sledding, but you can't find the sleds. Acceptable substitutes include...

a) trash can lids.
b) serving platters.
c) discarded pieces of metal roofing.
d) the cat's litter box.

The answer is *anything but d.* Sharp metal objects won't create an indoor mess. After a long night in the ER, the last thing you'll want to deal with is scattered cat feces.

6. How to cure frostbite

Some friends invite your kid to go ice skating. When she gets back, she "can't feel" her toes. You...

a) immerse her feet in warm water for thirty minutes.
b) rub her toes between your warm hands.
c) have her sit near the toasty fireplace.
d) sing a robust version of "I Told You So" by Randy Travis.

The correct answer is *a, b,* or *c* and *d.* She doesn't love your singing, but next time, maybe she'll take your advice and wear warmer socks.

Reminder! Solitaire is a great winter game for kids. It involves a little bit of math, and zero effort from you.

✻ CHAPTER 36 ✻

Early Release (a.k.a. Extra Torture): Fighting Back Against Two-Hour School Days

The standard American school day is eight hours long. This schedule would be easy for parents to remember, if it wasn't constantly switched it up. Like one day a week, the day is five hours long. And every other month, plus grade-reporting days, it's two hours long. In some districts, they even manage to fit in a couple of one-hour days. One hour of school is the *perfect* amount of time for kids to walk in, change their shoes, ask to get a drink of water, and leave again. And just enough time for you to shoot a tiny bit of heroin before picking them up.

For reasons that parents are not meant to understand—and have to do with either the federal requirements, bargaining agreements, Earth's orbit around the sun, or synthetic hormones in milk—there is no standard American school day. Since a tiny bit of heroin won't actually help you cope with their jackweed schedule, your hodgepodge of mom solutions to this problem needs to be just as creative, contingent, and confusing as the school calendar itself.

1. **Don't give up.**
   This is not a directive from the gun lobby about packing heat in schools. It's a metaphor about volunteering. Many parents help out in their children's classrooms, lunchrooms, or libraries. Maybe you run a program for the PTO that requires you to collate papers in the boiler room

because the school can't afford to give you a legitimate work space. That's cool. Taxes are a pretend thing, anyway, right? Just don't make the mistake of doing *any* of this free civic shit on an early-release day. Tempting as it may be to spend your only free hour volunteering because "you're already there," you're *bigger* than that boiler room. Almost literally. Take a walk, grab a coffee, get an oil change. Sit outside and breathe oxygenated air. Do anything but martyr yourself to the early-release crusade.

2. **Practice childcare solidarity.**
   Put all the early-release days in your calendar at the beginning of the year, then ask another mom if she'd like to alternate swapping kids. Cooperative parenting has a long and proud history. Hippies organize collective childcare programs in their neighborhoods. So do kibbutzim, casinos, and polygamous religious compounds. When those kids become Republicans later in life, it will have nothing to do with their feral, unregulated childhoods. The best part of early-release co-parenting is that there's no pressure to make the playdate productive, or even fun. The other mom doesn't give half a shit what her kid does. If he wastes the whole afternoon playing Geometry Dash and calling it "math," you're off the hook. Thanks, school board.

3. **Switch with your ex.**
   It's a widely known fact that dads never read class bulletins, PTO announcements, or school calendars. They avoid reading that shit on purpose. Of course they do. How else could they manage to look completely innocent when they miss it? *What? I didn't hit the Scholastic Book Fair this year!? Nobody told me!* You can work their ignorance in your favor, though. At the start of

the school year, send your ex-husband a note explaining that you'd like to change the custody arrangement to accommodate your "travel schedule." From now on, you will take Fridays if he takes every fourth Wednesday, a few random Mondays, and the second Thursday in January. He'll go for this because, you know, he's a big TGIF guy. Fridays are his favorite extramarital-affair day. Also, the dude has NO idea that Wednesdays are early-release. Get your lawyers to type it up. That way, if he complains later, you can act like a dumb prick. *What? Nobody told me!*

4. **Take heroic action.**
   You're never going to change the school system through civil disobedience, loud protesting, or even quiet conversation. Let's face it: If the people in charge of education wanted your input, they wouldn't have put something called "BBQ veggie riblets" on the hot lunch menu. But there are other ways to heroically resist your parental oppression. Try "forgetting" your kid. Teachers and office staff don't get to go home on early-release days. When you finally get to the school, be apologetic. Look confused. Then share this resistance strategy with your friends. If enough parents forget to pick up their kids on Wednesdays, maybe the principal will start an early-release afterschool program. If not, at least you got to the gym.

5. **Go on a hunger strike.**
   Nobody at your child's school cares whether or not you're starving yourself for justice. As long as you pay your field trip fees and send in snow boots, in fact, nobody cares about you at all. But then, don't let them take any credit when your new "early-release diet" becomes a hugely popular fad. Every day the school lets your kid go home

early, you stop eating. Given how many days this occurs, you'll be a size 4 by Easter. For extra weight loss, work in some calisthenics in the boiler room.

Reminder! If you have a flexible workplace, you could bring your early-released child to work. This may keep you from being fully productive. Don't worry. You will simply be fulfilling the gender stereotype your male colleagues already believe.

✻ CHAPTER 37 ✻

Holiday Tipping: Handing Out Money for Baby Jesus

Celebrating the holidays is a bit like getting a flu shot. They come every year, whether you're ready or not. They're a little painful. And you better get on top of it *early*, so you don't end up with bronchitis when the kids are home for winter break.

The real shot in the arm over the holidays, though, is the shopping. After buying specialty olive oil for distant relatives, you spice some nuts for the neighbors who stopped over with fruit bread, and then find something festive, inoffensive—and cheaper than fifteen dollars—for your office Secret Santa. Let's hope they fucking like fruit bread.

If you have school-age kids, early December is also when you get **the email**. That friendly note of reminder from Classroom Representative Mom, whom you've never met but who's already in your contact list because she's obsessed with helping. Her subject line says, "Time to get a holiday gift for the most awesome person we know!" No, she's not talking about the Israeli guy at the mall who gives you three free minutes in the massage chair. Or the couple down the street who came by and introduced themselves as your new "gaybors." They do seem awesome. But in this case, she's talking about the teacher.

TEACHER GIFTS ARE GLORIFIED TIPS.

It's customary during the holidays for people to *exchange* gifts. Even your husband knows this custom, and he's the guy who single-handedly keeps UPS in business by paying rush rates for overnight shipping on Christmas Eve. When we issue a gift in only one direction, it's usually for services rendered. This is known as a *tip*. People in this category include newspaper deliverers, dog sitters, hair stylists, and—in bigger cities, where the real rich people live—doormen. You don't shop for these folks because you necessarily love them or are related to them through marriage, or even because they are exceptional at their jobs. You're basically paying them off so they don't leave your packages—or house pets—in an abandoned warehouse.

There is one major exception to this golden rule of palm greasing: teachers. If your kid was a little bit more like a package—or a house pet—you could just hand the teacher an envelope full of cold, hard cash and be done with it. But because you cherish your kid with a depth of feeling that you supposedly don't feel about your labradoodle, you have to tip the teacher, but pretend like you're not.

It's not that you *don't* appreciate the teachers. You value every minute they spend with your child. In fact, you wish they could work their magic seven days a week, twelve months a year. But if it were just about *appreciation*, you could demonstrate gratitude in a hundred different, nonmaterial ways. You could sharpen more motherfucking pencils. You could volunteer to read books to the boys, so the girls could concentrate once in a while. You could volunteer in the lunchroom and scrape exploded ketchup packets off the floor, because that's the most obvious thing to do with your PhD. But that's not how it works, lunch ladies. The teachers need you to get your shit together so they receive gestures of holiday gratitude that have real market value.

EVERYONE IS A CHRISTIAN AT CHRISTMAS.

Americans celebrate a vast diversity of special cultural days. Indian people may celebrate Diwali. African American people may celebrate Kwanzaa. Jewish people may celebrate Hanukkah, which is a lot like Kwanzaa except it has different candles. When it comes to teacher gifts, however, it doesn't matter what religion you practice. Or what religion your kid's teacher practices. Eleven months a year, your son's fifth-grade teacher might sit cross-legged on a tree stump and meditate on Zen Buddhist sayings like *Calamity and fortune are two sides of the same coin*, but this is no time to be politically correct. You'll get plenty of that shit when your academic relatives come for Christmas dinner. Unless your kid goes to a special ethnic or religious school, "the holidays" means Christmas, and Christmas means *presents*. Those Tibetan singing bowls ain't cheap.

GIVE WITH THE GROUP, THEN SECRETLY GIVE MORE.
Many schools follow a tradition of collective giving. Shared gifts are classy and ethical. They allow all families to participate, regardless of their individual financial means. They set a good moral example for kids to follow, which they will do right up until they leave college and discover how the real world works.

Classroom Representative Mom will give you this helpful moral lecture in her email. But then she'll give the group gift to the teacher *by herself*. Of course she will. That bitch is helpful, but she's not Mother Theresa. You expect her to do all that organizational work simply out of the kindness of her heart? Nuh-uh. For your own kid's sake, you now need to level the appreciation-showing playing field. Contribute to the group gift, but put a little bit of cash aside so you can slip the teacher a more personalized present too. You may doubt this strategy, feel guilty about it, or worry that your secrecy will make the teacher feel uncomfortable. Not a chance. Teachers are nice people. Some are even Zen Buddhists. But they're not monks.

NOBODY WANTS A HOMEMADE GIFT.
Teachers aren't like the rest of us. They don't turn on the TV in the middle of the school day, unless they can pass it off as a science program. They don't give the kids an independent assignment, take a nap at their desk, and wake up twenty

minutes later with drool on their chin. They don't send kids into the basement to play because they're sick of hearing them talk. But if you imagined that teachers' good behavior meant they wanted a homemade gift, then you are not familiar with the term "legal compliance." Teachers follow these rules because they're required by law, not because they want a book of original haiku from a first grader. Where do you expect her to put a lopsided piece of pottery? Is there something about her wardrobe that suggests she's a sloppy hoarder? If not, get your kid to decorate a wine bag. That way, she can throw the homemade part away and still enjoy a decent gift.

Reminder! If your child's teacher specifically asks you not to give her a holiday gift, respect her wishes. But don't hold your breath. This is just about as likely as you canceling Mother's Day because your children are the only gift you need. They *are* a gift. But so is jewelry.

If You Want to Say Thanks with a Gift Card, Don't Say It with One That's Cheap, Half-Used, or Empty

Gift cards have become very popular in recent years. And that makes sense. Gift cards are basically cash tips that seem more personal because they have the word *gift* written on them. Want the perfect gift for the Buddhist guy who loves bowl music? Gift card from iTunes. What about the middle-aged ESL teacher who just got divorced? Gift card to a local spa. How about the music teacher with celiac disease who never, *ever* calls on your kid? Gift card to Olive Garden. He may or may not find something to eat there, but guess what, asshole? Everyone feels left out sometimes.

The tricky thing about gift cards is that, unlike chocolate, wine, and regifted fruit bread, they put a precise price tag on your appreciation. You might feel like you're tricking them with the word *gift*, but its value is actually right on the magnetic strip. Your daughter's teacher forgave you for sending her to school with seventy-one unsharpened pencils. She didn't yell at you about the high fever that mysteriously flared up six to eight hours into the school day. But she will *never* forget when she used your gift card for a few personal items at Target, and the register clerk had to void the small box of tampons. To make sure you don't send the wrong message about your appreciation, here is a high-level overview of what gift card values mean to various recipients.

TEACHER

$50: We appreciate you and love that our kid is in the highest math group.

$25: We appreciate you but wish our kid was in the highest math group.

$10: We don't really like you but feel bad our kid puked on the math room carpet.
$5: The principal blocked our room transfer. Enjoy a sandwich.

HAIRSTYLIST
$50: The color looks great. So glad I found your salon.
$25: I always love the color, mostly like the cuts.
$10: Supercuts costs more than this, hint, hint.
$5: Enjoy a cup of coffee while you fuck up someone else's hair.

NEWSPAPER DELIVERY PERSON
$50: The paper's always on the doorstep on time. I'm so well-informed in the morning.
$25: It occasionally lands in the bushes, but at least it's bagged up and dry.
$10: I feel bad you can't afford college, but maybe find a job you're good at.
$5: I saw you run into my mailbox. This is why people use the Internet.

GYMNASTICS TEACHER
$50: Thanks for being an awesome role model. Tumbling forever!
$25: Loved seeing her floor routine. Girl power!
$10: She cried for a week after she didn't make the team.
$5: You're a bitch and a diva, and we're switching her to ice hockey.

DOORMAN
$500: We adore you and can't live without you.
$250: We could live without you, but we do need that dry cleaning.
$100: You'd get more if you occasionally got off your phone.
$50: Uh, hi, the door? It's literally in your job title.

✻ CHAPTER 38 ✻

How to Make a Holiday Card That Isn't Ugly, Obscene, or Otherwise Inappropriate

God bless those moms who send out their holiday cards in the first week of December. Not only do they contribute to a more festive holiday season, but also when their cards arrive that early, they give the rest of us half a shot of sending ours out in time for New Year's, Eastern Orthodox Christmas—or Presidents' Day, *for sure.*

It's heartwarming to hear from faraway friends who send beautiful cards in a timely fashion. And let's face it. If holiday cards are a big part of seasonal giving, those people are giving *way* more than you are. But even if your holiday card is late, it could probably be so much worse.

* **Don't show that.** That may be a great shot of you on the beach. You were obviously working out back then. You should be proud of those guns. But you are also wearing a string bikini that you have no business wearing outside your backyard fertility hammock. And this card is going to your *boss.* Unless you want her husband to start referring to you as Nurse Cleavage, choose another photo. Holiday cards are no place for boobs, butts, sexy pregnant bellies, or—ahem, parents with their own spectrum issues—naked kids in the bathtub.

* **Whoa—too much holy.** Everyone knows that holiday cards are a tradition that stretches back to biblical times.

But unless you live on a religious compound and share your baby daddy with other brainwashed people, you probably know people from various faiths and religious backgrounds. Some of the folks in your address book don't necessarily believe that you drink someone's actual blood at church, or that shrimp cocktail will scar your soul. Identify your holiday if the spirit moves you. Send a thoughtful blessing. A dove in a ray of sunlight, maybe, or a rainbow. One of the great things about America is that you have the legal right to spend money on ugly shit like that. But keep it mellow. Any verse that includes the phrases GOD CHOSE US, PRAISE ALLAH, or ONWARD, CHRISTIAN SOLDIERS should probably stay in the tribe.

* **The scary personal reveal.** It's so great when people have time to include a friendly note in their holiday cards. It's updating friends on their residential whereabouts, special travel experiences, and big changes in their family life. Keep in mind that it's a holiday card, though, not a diary entry. Or an Alcoholics Anonymous meeting. Personal details you should *not* feel comfortable discussing in a holiday card include: the digestive health of your husband, the kids' new ADHD medications, the gruesome death of your backyard chickens, non-humorous references to how much you hate your job, adult children left at the altar, and ANY personal failings expressed through words like *bankruptcy*, *stalking*, or *registered sex offender*. And listen up, proud mamas. That big picture of your kid's trophy is nice. But a long narrative about their successful college entrance exams? That is *literally* why we drink.

* **Don't flaunt not-your-own-family.** It's totally fine to send out a picture of your kids with their grandparents because you have an outstanding shot of them making a

human pyramid at the family reunion. Also, grandparents are allowed to send pictures of anyone in the family, because it's all their genetic material. They giveth, and they taketh away. But that picture of your college buddies at the football game is an unofficial violation of holiday-card copyright. Just because you are also in the picture and you got those tickets from your boss doesn't make it kosher. Nobody gives a shit that you're popular or have good bennies. Also, random people will confuse your card recipients; they'll just think you got remarried. If you want to make other people envious of your social life, friend them on Facebook over the holiday break.

* **Don't flaunt your own family.** You've done an awesome job keeping portrait photographers gainfully employed. But real talk, photo-shoot moms. When you schedule a professional photo shoot *just for the holidays* and send everyone you've ever met one of your extra-heavy-stock cards that cost ten dollars a pop and accordions out to display your kids in forty-two adorable poses, you've gone too far. Now it just seems like you have something to hide/prove. If your card is so fancy and awesome that your kid could use it to get hired as a child actor, it's time to scale it back. People love you, and they love your kids. But not enough to want to see them smiling, laughing, acting like goofballs, duck-faced, and gazing into the distance—all in the same damn outfits—over and over and over.

Reminder! If it's already New Year's and you haven't gotten around to doing the holiday card, you may as well wait until February when the prices go down. Why doesn't anybody exchange Easter cards anymore?

✻ CHAPTER 39 ✻

New Year's Resolutions for Moms Who Can (Maybe) Do a Little Bit Better

New Year's resolutions only succeed if you are *realistic*. If you never exercise, for example, don't resolve to sign up for the Ironman. You'll either drown or choke on your own vomit, or both. If you never eat leafy greens, don't sign up for a weekly delivery from Leafy Greens Farm. It will just rot into kale liquid in your veggie drawer. Similarly, if you discourage your kid from practicing violin—because you can't stand the sound of horsehair scraping across metal—don't sign her up for youth symphony. Fact is, you may not have the stamina to raise a child prodigy. If Yo-Yo Ma had been your kid, he'd have been out in the street every night playing kick ball.

Set yourself up for success, moms. Pick one or two resolutions from the list below. Don't be too hard on yourselves. You can (maybe) do (just a little bit) better.

1. Get the kids to school on time, every day. Or less late. Three days.

2. Make meals with food groups other than cheese, tomato sauce, and pizza crust. Twice a week, for example, add onions or pepperoni.

3. Look at each new app your kid wants before you approve it. Unless it's educational. Or free.

4. If you're singing a Taylor Swift song at the top of your lungs on the sidewalk and your daughter begins to cry from embarrassment, stop doing it. Then use it later as emotional blackmail.

5. Don't automatically tell the kids to call their dad when they ask for a ride to the movies, unless he lives across town with his new family, in which case put him on speed dial.

6. If you can't say anything nice to your kids, say nothing at all. This pertains to any and all discussions of their mismatched outfits, their school projects, and the question "Do you like the picture I just drew?"

7. Never let your kids play at a friend's house where an unemployed uncle lives in the basement. Unless the mom is there, or the uncle is the only grown-up who's awake.

8. Don't say the words "breast buds." Just don't. Ever.

9. Take the kids to an art museum once a week. Or at least every six to eight weeks, so they have somewhere safe to sit while you're getting a facial.

10. Pay closer attention to your kid's health complaints. Your son might be "hypersensitive" and "weak," but he also might have the flu.

11. Teach the kids how to fish, farm, and hunt. If you live in a city, have them learn those skills on *Minecraft*.

12. Make a concerted effort not to fall asleep while reading to the kids at night because you've had a rough day at work and/or you drank too much beer.

13. Drink less beer.

14. Get off the phone *before* your kid pokes a wasp nest with a stick, not *after*. UNLESS he does that while you're on the phone with your cable service or an airline, in which case, stay on hold and tell him to *run*.

15. Calling your kids by the dog's name is fine. But giving them treats to fetch you a beer might be weird.

16. Make your kids complete every chain letter they receive so they grow up knowing how to identify—and profit from—a Ponzi scheme.

17. Don't swear around, about, or at your children. If you can't follow these rules, just don't do the last one.

18. Establish a money jar to penalize yourself for every time you swear around or about your children.

19. Give the swearing jar's contents to charity when it's full.

20. Stop stealing from the swearing jar to pay for field trips, hot lunch accounts, and parking meters. If you need to empty it completely—because you need money for beer and pizza—refill it the next day, or as soon as your kids notice.

Reminder! If your kids are old enough to know what New Year's means, they may want to stay up and ring in the New Year. Turn on the news six hours early. As soon as the ball drops in Madrid, it's time for bed!

Head Lice DOs and DON'Ts

* **DO** take it seriously when the school sends home a lice notice. When the nurse writes that "one or more" students have lice, the classroom reading carpet is already infested.

* **DO** check your child's head for lice as soon as possible, so it doesn't spread in your home. If you find bugs, use any and every homeopathic remedy you can find, including tea tree oil, mayo, and olive oil. When those don't work, shower your child in poison.

* **DO** send your kid back to school the next day, whether the lice are gone or not. Why the fuck not? Some other parent obviously did.

* **DO** tell your kid to stay away from classmates whose hair smells weird, especially if they are Caucasian. This may sound discriminatory. But everyone knows that lice, like gentlemen, prefer blondes.

* **DON'T** believe any website that says people who get lice aren't dirty. If there was no link between lice and hygiene, those websites wouldn't also tell you to clean every fucking thing in your house when your kid gets lice.

* **DON'T** immediately freak out when your own head starts to itch. Phantom lice is a real condition. But just in case, shower yourself with poison.

* **DON'T** let your infested kid hang out with a friend, unless you inform the parents of his condition. If they find out from someone else—or their kid gets lice—they will naturally assume your family is dirty.

* **DON'T** assign the task of lice-checking to anyone else, especially a husband. This is a man who goes to the grocery store with a list and *still comes home with the wrong items*. You can't Y-chromosome this shit.

* CHAPTER 40 *

Cabin Fever Is Real: What to Do If It Happens to You

Weather reports sound like soap operas these days. *Freezing temperatures and eighty inches of snow?* You're always like, *AS IF. That sounds like the apocalypse!* Only when the storm hits do you get the hysteria. The "storm of the century" started as icy rain, then turned to snow. It snowed for twenty-four hours straight, sideways, then grapefruit-sized hail started coming down like it was being shot out of a pitching machine. By the time it was over, your elm tree had fallen into the driveway and your front door was buried under a snowdrift. That's when you got the REALLY bad news: School's canceled.

When people plan for big storms, they usually focus on life-support systems, like clean water and flashlights with batteries. Staying alive is great and everything, but if you're a mom, you have other shit to worry about. You need to worry about staying sane so that when they finally dig you out, they don't take your children away. You need an emergency kit of activities for distracting and entertaining your climate-changed kids.

MAKE YOUR OWN CRYSTAL RADIO.

The upside: This activity takes a lot of time, and if constructed properly, the radio is an awesome way to get news. The downside of this quick and easy DIY project is that it's not. Exactly none of the materials are lying around your house when you need them. Unless, of course, you have a sturdy plastic bottle, fifty feet of enamel-coated magnet wire, a hundred feet of insulated wire, an old-school telephone handset, a set of alligator jumpers, and a germanium diode. *Honey, didn't we get rid of that germanium diode at our last garage sale?* If you did hang on to the diode, use an ice pick for the holes and consider popping in a few machine screws for the platform. These are both great and extremely safe jobs for the kids. What better time than Armageddon to learn how to handle unstable voltage? Good luck!

MAKE BUTTER.

If the power company gets the electrical grid back online in less than a day, your dairy products won't sour. But if you're worried about it, make the cream last longer by turning it into butter. Kids love this activity! Hand each kid a mason jar or jelly jar with some heavy cream and a tight lid and tell them to start shaking their jars. Have them do this for at least two to three uninterrupted hours. The cream will actually turn into butter in about ten minutes. The rest of the time is just a way to tire out their arms so they don't punch each other.

HAVE FUN WITH CORKS.

A lot of moms save their corks when they open a bottle of wine. If you are one of those moms—and you drink a lot of wine—you have a lot of corks. Corks are great for crafting. Take out some wood glue and challenge the kids to make three-dimensional representations of the end of the world. Starter ideas include zombie attacks, fallen trees, looters, imaginary crystal radios, and cold cans of beans. There's no limit to their creativity, and no end to the supplies. Especially if you keep opening new bottles while they visualize their destruction.

GET BACK INTO FINGER KNITTING.

Remember how much your kids used to love finger knitting? Or loved it for five days before they outgrew it? Somewhere in your "crafting bin"—thanks Amazon Prime!—you still have twenty ziplock bags full of unused cotton loops. Have the kids work together to knit the longest rope they can make. Tell them to go fast, and pretend it's a matter of life or death. When the rope reaches twenty feet, tie one end to the foot of your bed and dangle the other end out your bedroom window. Point to whichever kid got the best grade in gym class. Now have him climb down the rope and go for help.

CREATE MASKING TAPE SIGNS.

This is a great alternative to knitting for those moms who have boys and/or recently threw away all the finger-knitting shit in a clutter-induced rage. Cut up an old cardboard box and get some rolls of masking tape. These are usually lying around somewhere in the basement, near the empty paint cans. Challenge the kids to "write" words with masking tape on the cardboard. This craft is educational and hones multiple skills at once, including spatial reasoning, physical coordination, and spelling. Fun spelling ideas include SEND HELP, SAVE US, and NEED NETFLIX. When they're done, hang their fun signs out a second-story window facing the street.

MAKE HOMEMADE PLAYDOUGH.

This kitchen game is good for snow days because it doesn't require an oven. Have your kids sit down at the table or kitchen island, as if they're being served breakfast. Mix the ingredients—flour, salt, food coloring, oil—and knead them together until a soft dough forms. When the playdough is ready, tell them to make shapes of their favorite foods. *Now eat them all up, kids. Nom. Nom. That's the closest thing you're gonna get to a hot meal until the snowplow rolls through!*

PLAY BOOKSHELF CHARADES.

For this game, every person in the family chooses a book from the living room shelf. Don't show it to anyone else! Using the signs and gestures from classical charades—ear pulling, finger counting, etc.—take turns acting out the title of each book. If you're playing by candlelight, everyone will look a bit like a ghost. Depending on the ages of your kids, how many days you've been stranded, and how much food you have left, you may want to remove the following titles before you play: *The Exorcist*, *American Psycho*, *The Silence of the Lambs*, *Rosemary's Baby*, *The Amityville Horror*, *Carrion Comfort*, *The Girl Next Door*, *We Need to Talk About Kevin*, and *Hell House*.

SURF THE DARK WEB.

The Dark Web is a part of the Internet that people access with special authorizations and encryption. There's a lot of scary stuff on it that isn't for kids, including porn, infidelity sites, fraud, and drug dealing. Some of these sites may include pictures of your kids you posted on Facebook and thought were secure because you put that fake legal disclaimer on your news feed. But guess what? Since you have no power and your computer is dead, there's no danger of your kids finding any of it. Or anything else. Your Web, like everything else in your house, is literally dark. Yay, parental controls!

Reminder! If your computer has a little battery power left, see if you can find the REAL Dark Web. Snowstorms are the perfect time to find out if your husband is dinking around behind your back. If it turns out he's submitted his name to a marital cheating site, don't leave him for lying. Leave him for being a complete fucking idiot.

⁕ CHAPTER 41 ⁕

If You Can Survive February, You Can Survive Anything. Even Valentine's Day.

If antidepressants had a "season," it would be that chunk of time between winter break and spring break, when nobody has anything to do. Sure, there are some indie film festivals taking place here and there. People in New Orleans remove their clothing in exchange for plastic beads. People from Michigan drive down to Florida, where fifty degrees feels hot. But the rest of the country just has school and winter and Presidents' Day. And since exactly nobody celebrates George Washington's birthday anymore, everyone just gets depressed instead.

Then it's Valentine's Day. V-Day. VD. What is the secret to surviving this February sap fest? Mock it, ignore it, or—better yet—outsource it to people who are nicer than you. Namely, the teachers.

V-DAY WAS ORIGINALLY ABOUT TORTURE.

Valentine's Day is notorious for making single people want to crawl under a rock and read Baudelaire. The more you learn about its history, however, the more you want to skip the depressing French poetry and just kill yourself. Valentine's Day has been traced back to an early Roman feast called Lupercalia, during which men whipped naked women with animal skins to make them more fertile. Just in case that didn't work, they also "had sex" with them, which may have been a Lupercalian euphemism for rape. The Catholic Church, skeptical of this fertility treatment, downgraded Valentine's Day into a commemoration of tortured martyrs. Instead of Roman women, Saint Valentine took one for the team. It wasn't until European romantics came along—and reinterpreted V-Day as a celebration of love and courtship—that anyone associated the holiday with things like hearts and sweets and cupids.

AMERICANS MADE IT STUPID AND FAKE.

Several hundred years after the Europeans transformed V-Day into a hetero-patriarchal celebration of love, the Hallmark company began mass-producing "Valentines," in the form of greeting cards. Where French people had drafted personal love notes, Americans turned V-Day into yet another drugstore holiday that people cared about only if it wasn't properly observed. Single women, for example, concluded that if their boyfriends did NOT buy them a diamond and propose marriage on February 14, then their love was hollow and they'd gotten themselves pregnant for nothing. Husbands concluded that if they FORGOT to buy dime-store chocolate roses, their wives would put them in the doghouse/refuse to have sex. Wives pretended to mind but really didn't because, February. They'd rather just sleep.

WHAT HAS VALENTINE'S DAY DONE FOR MOMS LATELY?

We get you, single ladies. Your womb wants you to put a ring on it. But you should know that once you get that ring and squeeze out that pup, Valentine's Day just morphs into a new kind of monster—a monster made of lacy white paper doilies and red construction paper. Overnight, you'll develop guilt about missing the segment where Martha Stewart taught Grover how to make heart-shaped cupcakes. Why *did* you miss that? Because you had to clean decomposed food out of your veggie drawer? Priorities, priorities. But you can redeem yourself when you go to the dentist on Martin Luther King Jr. Day. Pick up *literally any magazine* and read an article about decorating your kids' lunchboxes with paper flowers, cutting hearts into their peanut butter and jelly sandwiches, or using chopsticks and rubber bands to make "heart-boiled eggs." Because who doesn't have time to run out and grab a wide variety of kitchen implements—in various shapes and sizes—and custom-design their children's meals? Everyone knows that just **making** the kids a nutritious breakfast isn't fun-loving enough. Or loving enough. Or enough. Heart-boiled eggs, bitches.

DO LESS.

So what's a craft hater to do? Can we just sit around and joke about how crafty people sometimes go to prison? Not really. Because Martha Stewart did her time, and then got right back to her life's mission of torturing us with origami. Luckily, television and magazines are not like the Internet; you can pretend they don't exist. If you do your best to mock V-Day, but your kid goes rogue and asks you for a cereal box to make special cardboard valentines, point her toward the recycling and cross your fingers that your partner finished off the nutty granola. When your little guy takes out a class list because he wants to make valentines for everyone, praise him for his inclusiveness but ignore his characteristic lack of follow-through. It's cold outside. So tired. And seventeen out of twenty-three is pretty damn close.

THE TEACHER'S GOT THIS.

Why is your cynical, lazy attitude about this holiday acceptable? Because making heart-shaped food on Valentine's Day is a lot like sending your kid to school with dry mittens. If you don't do it well, or do it at all, the teacher will save your ass. Not only that, but the teacher will almost certainly do a better job than you would have. In this VD-infected world—where we have to choose between prefab cards from Costco or unrealistic craftiness—schoolteachers are like the classical Europeans.

They are the Old World romantics who still believe in simple, messy, recycled, handcrafted love notes. To an elementary schoolteacher, Valentine's Day is about only two things: (1) having fun and (2) being nice. That's why teachers encourage kids to write cards, help kids affix small candies to floppy paper with Scotch tape, and *don't* help them spell words correctly. Teachers know something Martha Stewart doesn't: It's not about the art—it's about the heart.

P.S. YOUR KIDS WILL BE FINE.

Ultimately, your kids are not the ones foisting unreasonable expectations about Valentine's Day on you. Those expectations are coming from your dentist, and the crafty women of Cell Block 4. Do kids love heart-shaped cupcakes if someone has time to make them? Totally. Do they love glittery frosting, especially because they don't have to clean it up? Indeed. But they also like drawing shapes, using scissors, writing their friends' names in bubble letters, folding papers a hundred times until they're really small, and passing secret notes to each other with simple messages like I LOVE YOU. Kids, like teachers, are sweeter and less cynical than you are. For them, digging an old cereal box out of the trash and decorating it with construction paper so that it can be filled with misspelled valentines is a pretty damn good day. Do your kids a favor: Get out of the way, and let them school you on what love means.

Reminder! Even the most dedicated, passionate, and loving parents feel like they are doing a terrible job sometimes. Keep the passion, dump the guilt. Happy Valentine's Day, Sh*tty Moms!

Real-Life Valentines to Help You Survive February

Valentines from kids to moms

* I love my mommy because she reads books to me. She also works on a computer. And has a black car.
* I love my mommy because sometimes, she gives me great snacks.
* This Valentine's coupon is good for a fun day, only with me.
* I hope this is the best valentine you ever had. Sorry it's backward and upside down.
* This Valentine's coupon is good for a trip to France.
* Happy Valentine's Day to a sooper mommy. You are the best mommy of my life.

Valentines from kids to other kids

* It's Valentine's Day. Happy Valentine's Day. I can't believe it's already Valentine's Day!
* How are you? I was rooting for the Packers in the Super Bowl and they're the team who won.
* You are a good friend. I like how you read.
* You are a good friend, even though you never talk to me.
* I don't know who you are. Happy Valentine's Day.
* I really like the shirt your mom got you with the dinosaur on it. Happy Valentine's Day.
* Hi, it's me, Benny! Happy Valentine's Day. What did you get for Christmas? Your friend, Benny.
* What do you do at recess? Do you ever hide ice chunks and store them?
* You are so, so nice to everyone. I really, really like you. Are you going to Sam's barbecue?
* I love you so much. Do you love me? Why not?

AFTERWORD

Because Love Is a Twelve-Letter Word

Having read/skimmed this whole book, you may still have questions. Like, why do moms need so much advice, anyway? Why do we feel self-conscious if we don't cry on the school playground or make heart-boiled eggs on Valentine's Day? Why are women their own worst critics, when criticizing husbands comes so much more naturally?

Science can't answer all of those questions, so we'll just throw out some fake theories. Most regular moms, for example, have infinite love for their children. Yet the number of ways we can reasonably be expected to demonstrate our love on any given day—to our kids and everyone else—is much smaller. Research suggests that number is about thirty-three.

There's nothing wrong with thirty-three. If you received thirty-three presents on Mother's Day, for example, it would be a windfall. You'd probably get a bunch of IOUs, a houseplant, French toast, a few sassy dishtowels, and maybe even some jewelry. But thirty-three is just a regular number. Infinity is a lot bigger than regular numbers. That's why we always feel bad. Thanks, Albert Einstein.

If you remember one piece of advice from this book, remember that love is a twelve-letter word. No, it's not *streetwalker* or an *undergarment*, or a *gynecologist*. Love is related to all of those words in a variety of slightly creepy ways, but the word you want is *motherfucker*. That's right. Love is a MOTHERFUCKER. All we can do is try to show it who's boss. Get out there, Sh*tty Moms, parent the shit out of your kids, and kick next year's ass!

ACKNOWLEDGMENTS

So many incredible people helped to make this book happen. First, thank you and XOXO to our agent, Yfat Reiss Gendell. She brought us together, kept us on track, supported our talents, managed our tantrums, and did all of it with panache, toughness, composure, charm, and hotness. Thank you to the entire Foundry Literary & Media group, especially the hard work of Jessica Felleman, Kirsten Neuhaus, Sara DeNobrega, Michon Vanderpoel, Michelle Hammon, and Richie Kern.

We are also humbled by the artistry and creative talent that sustained this project at Abrams. We are indebted to our wise and patient editor, Rebecca Kaplan, for clarifying our words, illuminating our vision, and setting a lofty bar of professional excellence. We are likewise grateful for the contributions of the brilliant Abrams team, including Sally Knapp, Zack Knoll, Steve Tager, Claire Bamundo, Mary Wowk, John Gall, Danielle Young, Christoph Niemann, and publisher Michael Sand.

Mary Ann Zoellner:

To my husband, Alexander, and my two daughters, Zurielle and Arabella, who still blush when they say the word Sh*tty—love y'all to the moon and back. To all my siblings, thanks for your laughter, love, and support (even when I'm being all shady).

Alicia Ybarbo:

To Mark, Jack, and Lucy—your smiles and laughter give me the energy to take on any challenge. I love you all very much.

Erin Clune:

Thanks to everyone who shared their stories with me, and to my writing support squad of Melissa, Heather, Renata, Tara, Justine, Jordan, Alisyn, Alivia, and Barriques coffee. To my extended family, thank you for everything. To Mike, Emmy, and Molly—I love you infinitely, and Pluto is *totally* a planet.

To our moms—Ann Knight, Irene Ybarbo, and Constance Clune

Published in 2016 by Abrams Image
An imprint of ABRAMS.

Library of Congress Control Number: 2015949277

ISBN: 978-1-4197-1404-7

Editor: Rebecca Kaplan
Designer: Danielle Young
Production Manager: True Sims

Printed and bound in the United States
10 9 8 7 6 5 4 3 2 1

ABRAMS
THE ART OF BOOKS SINCE 1949
115 West 18th Street
New York, NY 10011
www.abramsbooks.com

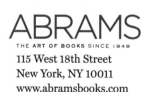